THE ART OF
SOLDERING FOR JEWELRY MAKERS
TECHNIQUES AND PROJECTS

THE ART OF
SOLDERING FOR JEWELRY MAKERS
TECHNIQUES AND PROJECTS

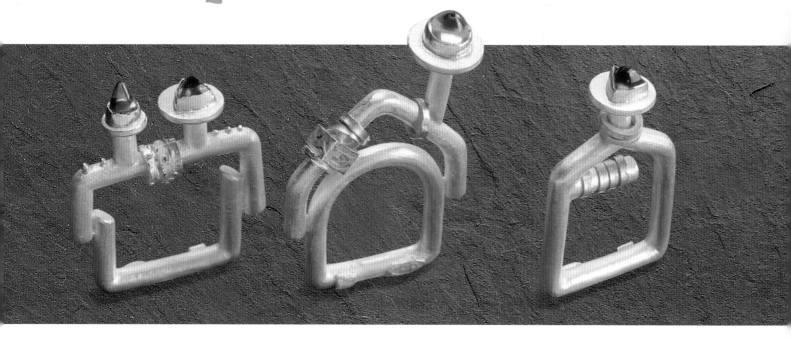

Wing Mun Devenney

BARRON'S

A QUARTO BOOK

This edition published in
North America in 2013 by
Barron's Educational Series, Inc.

All inquiries should be addressed to:
Barron's Educational Series, Inc.
250 Wireless Boulevard
Hauppauge, NY 11788
www.barronseduc.com

ISBN: 978-1-4380-0263-7

Library of Congress Control Number: 2013940031

QUAR:DSJ

Conceived, designed, and produced by
Quarto Publishing plc
The Old Brewery
6 Blundell Street
London N7 9BH

Project editor: Lily de Gatacre
Art editor and designer: Susi Martin
Copy editor: Claudia Martin
Photographer: Phil Wilkins
Proofreader: Caroline West
Indexer: Ann Barrett
Picture Researcher: Sarah Bell

Creative director: Moira Clinch
Publisher: Paul Carslake

Color separation in Hong Kong by
Modern Age Repro House Limited
Printed in China by 1010 Printing International Limited

9 8 7 6 5 4 3 2 1

Publisher's Note

Jewelry-making involves working with hot metals, cutting tools, and high
temperature burners, activities which are potentially hazardous and carried out
at your own risk. The guidelines laid down in this book on pages 10–11 on safe
working practices and workstations are important, and should be read and
followed carefully. Readers should also check their compliance with health
and safety legislation currently in force, and always follow manufacturers'
instructions, guidelines, and recommendations for using and storing tools and
equipment. Inform your insurance company if storing or using combustible gas
within or near an insured premises. The publisher accepts no liability for loss or
damage sustained in the course of using this book.

Contents

Author Foreword

Soldering techniques have remained relatively unchanged over time and, although there are advanced technologies available now, the principles of soldering continue much the same. The fact is that with very few tools, elaborate and complicated jewelry designs can be created by soldering. Unlike the threading and stringing of components, soldering finishes a piece completely—it joins metal parts together securely, allowing components to be fixed at almost any desired angle. There is no risk of pieces coming apart or becoming loose; it is a permanent connection and this is what makes it so magical and diverse. Joins of mixed metals and almost any shaped components are possible and allow the creation of endless designs. Furthermore, the soldering of fittings, such as stone settings or findings, allows the jewelry piece to incorporate non-metal materials such as gemstones, and permits the securing of the piece to the wearer.

This book is suitable for beginner jewelers who wish to learn about soldering, but additionally can be a valued reference book for those who are advanced jewelry makers. Divided into two sections, the first part of this book explores a variety of commonly used soldering techniques before progressing onto 15 individual step-by-step soldering projects. Each of the projects will apply skills learned from the techniques presented at the start of the book, allowing you to follow the instructions and create a selection of jewelry and accessory pieces. By adapting sizes and features from the projects, you can also tailor the pieces to your own designs and, hopefully, with the skills acquired, you can develop your own individual pieces.

I hope you, like I did, will discover the magic of soldering.

Wing Mun Devenney

About this Book

This book is organized into four chapters covering all you need to know about soldering. The opening two chapters teach you all you need to know to get started before you work your way through the techniques and projects.

. . . .

Be safe!
Being safe is the first and most important consideration: Follow the general health and safety instructions starting on page 10 and be guided by the specific instructions throughout the content.

Introduction pages, pages 8–19
An introduction to the art and craft of making hot connections and moving your jewelry-making to a new level. Includes a glorious gallery of work by leading makers who describe the soldering techniques they use.

Chapter 1: Getting Started in Soldering, pages 20–49
An introduction to the soldering process, from choosing a torch, understanding solders and fluxes, planning and preparation to different methods for holding small metal parts; these instructions apply to all soldering techniques. Includes a useful guide to how different metals respond to the soldering process.

Chapter 2: Key Soldering Techniques, pages 50–81
Organized with beginner techniques first, such as butt soldering, and leading to more challenging methods such as stick feed soldering. Here you will find detailed instructions and guidelines, including suggestions for how to use the various joins in your jewelry making.

Chapter 3: Post-Soldering Processes, pages 82–91
Follow protocols for cleaning and polishing your work for a truly professional finish.

Chapter 4: Projects, pages 92–153
Shown in step-by-step sequences, the construction of simple but beautiful jewelry pieces in Wing Mun Devenney's signature style. Each project comes complete with tools and materials lists, so you can assemble everything you need before you start, deconstructed views of the item of jewelry prior to assembly, with dimensions, and references back to the techniques chapter, so, if you need to find more detailed background information, you can easily do so.

From Chapter 2: Key Soldering Techniques

Guidelines
Overview of the procedure and order of work, including how to prevent errors and oversights.

Tools and materials
Tools are listed in the order you use them.

Skill level
On a scale of 1–3, with 1 being for beginners.

Finished examples
Carefully chosen pieces of jewelry relevant to the soldering technique by Wing Mun Devenney and other leading jewelry designers. In each case, caption provides information about the soldering process.

Enlarged details
Enlarged details of the process aid visual understanding.

From Chapter 4: Projects

Finished piece

Tools and materials
Tools are listed in the order you use them.

Skill level
On a scale of 1–3, with 1 being for beginners.

Techniques used
Cross references back to techniques used in the previous chapters.

Deconstructed view, pre-assembly
Components are shown actual size and dimensions are provided: Use this information to check the size of your components.

Materials
Materials specification

Note:
Imperial and metric measurements
When making a project, follow either metric OR imperial measurements. Some of the measurements given are very small, so it would be ideal to work from the metric measurements. All conversions given are approximate.

Introduction

To produce a piece of jewelry entirely from one component is almost impossible. Soldering, also known as silver brazing or hard soldering, is the most common process used by jewelers to join together metals permanently.

Cubist Ring
**Inness
Thomson**

There are a variety of methods of attaching components in jewelry making, such as rivets, screw systems, hinges, crimps, welds, wire or fiber knots, pins, and adhesives. Apart from the welding option, this selection of joins are called cold connections, as the process of joining the two parts is carried out without the application of heat. Cold connections can prevent damage to heat-sensitive materials and can join mixed materials or metals. Screw-type systems allow the piece to be disconnected or opened. But without soldering, only limited construction possibilities can be achieved. Soldering offers a strong, seamless, and clean method

Helix Rings
Faith Tavender

of joining metals. With the proper use of this technique, endless options and varied design opportunities are achievable.

Although soldering is a frequently applied technique, it can often be taken for granted and thought of as a by-product of the piece. A considerable number of jewelers have poor or little soldering knowledge and tend to place more importance on other jewelry techniques. All too often, this lack of understanding leads to mistakes, such as weak or poorly assembled joints, so it must be remembered that soldering is an important—if not the most critical—jewelry technique to possess.

Soldering can be challenging, but with practice a jeweler can master and develop their own style, as well as home in on particular techniques they prefer. Soldering requires patience, but the more you practice, the more expert you will become.

A Little History

There is evidence to suggest that soldering or bonding of metal to metal dates back to around 3000 B.C.E. in Sumer, before reaching areas such as Egypt, the Mediterranean, and farther afield. The use of soldering ran across products and was not exclusive to jewelry making. In fact, it is only in our modern day that metal workers are so separated: Historically, metal work encompassed jewelry as well as structural, decorative, and practical objects. Historically, the main types of metal joining were soft

soldering, hard soldering or brazing, eutectic soldering, and "casting on."

Soft soldering uses metal fillers, known as solder, with melting temperatures between 390 and 750°F (200–400°C) and consisting of metal alloys such as tin and lead. Today, this form of soldering is more commonly associated with plumbing work.

Hard soldering or brazing uses solders with higher melting temperatures, in excess of 1470°F (800°C). These solders have similar but lower melting points than the parent metal, which allows the join to be particularly strong. This is the form of soldering commonly used for jewelry construction today.

Eutectic soldering—which has many names, including diffusion, autogenous, colloidal, or chemical soldering—was in the past traditionally used for decorative purposes such as granulation and filigree designs. Today, it is still used for joining decorative pieces. Eutectic soldering uses no form of additional filler/solder. It works by painting the surface metal with a glue mixture of tragacanth gum and copper salts before applying decorative pieces, be it granules or fine wire detailing. When heated in the reducing atmosphere of a charcoal hearth, the tragacanth is burnt away, leaving the copper salt, which diffuses between the decorative granules or wire and the metal background (gold), joining the two surfaces together. Effectively, the diffusion of the copper oxide changes the gold surface into a solder alloy.

"Casting on" also does not require the use of solder. This procedure worked by creating a clay mold—for example, the handle of a knife around a pre-made bronze knife blade. Molten bronze was poured into the mold. Fusion between the handle and the blade immediately occurred. This process was used for a variety of components but was limited to bronze.

The fundamental factor that allows metal bonding to occur in soldering and brazing is heat. Today, we commonly use torches that function on a supply of gas and air or oxygen. These produce direct heat, which has to be applied in a manner that creates even heat distribution before solder will flow successfully. In the past, furnaces and ovens were often used for soldering. (They still are today in a mass-production environment.) Unlike soldering torches, furnaces and ovens produce indirect diffused heat. Historically, furnaces were constructed from clay and charcoal, with evidence to suggest the use of peat or dung in certain types of ovens. Furnaces—in particular those made from charcoal—offered a reducing atmosphere that meant levels of oxide formation were low, thus allowing solder to flow. This meant that fluxes were in less regular use than they are today. However, there is certainly evidence to suggest the use of fluxes made from substances like tartaric acid, derived from wine, which are mentioned in medieval literature.

Soldering Today

Today, there are a variety of torches available for metal workers, ranging from the more dated, bench-secured, swivel action torch, which functions on gas and is manually operated and flame controlled by the user's breath, through to hand-held atmospheric and mains or pressurized gas and air versions.

Relatively recent developments in technology mean that precision metal-bonding equipment, such as laser and PUK welders, has moved to the forefront of jewelry making. Laser welders work by melting the two adjoining metals with a laser beam, thus fusing them together. The laser pinpointing the join area is so concentrated that it does not disturb the surrounding areas, creating a focused and strong bond. Laser welders were originally invented for jewelers to repair claw settings where the work was fine and the heat generated had to be contained to avoid damage to the stone. Now the laser welder has been adopted by designers to create extremely detailed and elaborate designs that conventional soldering could not have achieved successfully.

TIG welders, which were initially invented for engineering operations such as welding vehicle parts together, were adopted for joining larger silversmith pieces. With the demand for a smaller version of the TIG came the introduction of a precision version, the PUK, which is a micro version of the TIG. The PUK pulse arc welder fuses metals together with an electric arch. The manufacturers of PUK welders claim that they work in almost the same way as laser welders but at a fraction of the cost. The preference of one for the other often comes down to the cost for an independent jeweler, and often neither is accessible outside a commercial or educational environment. However, for those metal workers and jewelers who have the opportunity to use them, the advantages of laser or PUK welders are that they allow the invisible and speedy joining of metals, strong joins, and no solders and fluxes. Both pieces of equipment allow the tacking of parts prior to soldering, relinquishing the set-up

Indian Summer
Suzan Rezac

process and reducing the risk of pieces or components falling apart. These benefits have provided many designers and makers with complicated construction possibilities that were impossible with conventional torch soldering.

Laser and PUK welders have changed jewelry production in many ways, and taken jewelry design and development to another level. However, the traditions of soldering with a torch continue, and nothing compares to the satisfaction of completing a jewelry piece that has been hand fabricated and soldered. There is no substitute for the anticipation of waiting for the glistening flow of solder as you control and direct it with a soldering torch. To witness the creation of a perfect solder seam is magical. This book will guide you to complete success in soldering.

Health and Safety

Health and safety is a vital consideration when working with heat, fire, and flammable or hazardous chemicals. This section guides you through the precautions you should take, and the equipment and techniques you should use, in order to minimize the risk of damage to yourself, your work, or your surroundings.

Area for Workshop and Soldering

Independent home jewelers often set up workshops in a spare room, garage, outhouse, or in a rented workshop. Workshops can be located in any area of your home, but consider where you will feel the most comfortable, if you will have access to good lighting, and whether you are close to electrical outlets for tools that require power. Ideally, the workbench and soldering area should be positioned near a wall, allowing the back of the soldering station to be free from flammable items. In addition, due to the use of certain chemicals during soldering, it is best to work in a well-ventilated area.

Heat-proof Equipment

Soldering must always be carried out against a suitable heat-proof background, both to protect the surrounding area and to allow optimum heat reflection. Heat-proof bricks and mats should always be used and ideally placed on a heat-proof turntable. The surrounding background should be clear, free from flammable objects, and also protected by a metal shield or cover.

Essential Fire Safety Equipment

Extinguishers and fire blankets should be suspended close at hand. The appropriate extinguishers and fire blankets should be sourced for the type of gas and substances that the jeweler chooses to have in their workshop. Fire experts should be contacted to offer safety advice, and supply health and safety guidelines.

Storing Torches

First of all, and most importantly: Always call on an expert to fit the parts of a torch together. They will know the procedures that ensure the torch is set safely. The expert will also be able to offer advice to ensure the torch is used correctly.

Any hand-held torches should be switched off when not in use. Torches that use gas and air, and have a pilot flame, should be hooked safely onto the workbench, away from flammable materials. When a torch is not in use, make sure that the safety flame is kept ignited. If it is not, gas will be released unsafely into the air. Therefore, it is wise to keep the torch away from open windows, which may allow a breeze that can extinguish the flame without you noticing.

Use protective eyewear.

Keep eyewash in the first-aid box.

Always remember that even when a torch has been switched off, the nozzle can still retain heat, so take care to avoid contact. Gas bottle torches that are not in use should always have the gas turned off at the canister. Be aware that insurance companies do not permit the use of many types of gas canisters and blow torches in homes. It is best to check with your insurance company before proceeding with the use of any types of gases and torches in your home.

Gas Canisters and Lighters

Gas canisters should be placed on a flat floor surface away from where they can easily be knocked, which could disconnect them from the hose pipe.

When lighting the flame, it is advisable to use friction lighters or matches rather than disposable cigarette lighters, as many of these are highly flammable. Matches should also be kept away from the flame when not in use. Of course, when you are igniting a torch, point the flame away from yourself.

Storage of Chemicals

Ensure all chemicals are stored in their original containers, as important and useful information will be stated on the packaging. It is best to keep all chemicals in a lockable cabinet that can be secured when they are not in use.

Suitable Clothing

When open flames are used, a jeweler should carefully consider their choice of clothing. Wear sleeveless clothing if possible, as you will instinctively pull away from heat on your skin but will be slower to notice burning on a piece of clothing. Loose clothing, especially sleeves, should be avoided. Wear an apron that will protect youand your clothing from falls and splashes of hot items or pickle solution.

Using Tweezers and Prongs

It is common sense always to use tweezers to lift heated parts, and it is advisable to do so even when a period has elapsed after soldering or heating. Very often a metal piece will retain the heat far longer than you would suspect from its cool appearance. It is all too easy to pick up items absentmindedly, not realizing the item is still hot or has perhaps become hot from the heat released off a recently used firebrick. Regardless of circumstances, always use tweezers to transfer soldered or heated pieces. In addition, keep a glass or ceramic container of cold water within easy reach of your soldering area for cooling of metals.

Hair Safety

Tie or pin back any loose hair to avoid contact with the flame. This is not only for safety reasons: It also allows the jeweler to have the best view for soldering.

Protective Eyewear

Appropriate eyewear should be worn when working with high-intensity heating equipment. Refer to user manuals for specific advice. Also remember to wear protective eyewear when using, or in close proximity to, pickle solution.

First-aid Equipment

A first-aid box should be close at hand in the workshop. Contained in the first-aid box should be a standard burns medical unit, an eye-wash kit, and other medical requirements a medical expert can advise on.

Running Cold Water

It is best to have running cold water in a workshop in order to treat any burns right away. If this is not possible, keep cool water close at hand in a ceramic or glass dish.

Lighting

A slightly darkened environment provides the optimum light conditions for soldering. The jeweler should use good strong lighting to prepare their parts prior to soldering, then dim the light source once the components have been set up. However, when the lights are dimmed, ensure the environment is lit enough for the safe use of equipment.

Equipment Maintenance

Remember to check and maintain all your equipment and machinery. It is ideal to have an annual inspection to ensure equipment is performing safely and at its best.

Working at the Jewelry Workshop

Finally, one of the most important factors to consider when you are working in a jewelry workshop, particularly during soldering, is to be alert and to have no distractions. If you are tired or distracted, not only will your work be affected but your safety could be at risk, too.

Design Gallery

For the independent designer jeweler, soldering is an important manufacturing technique. Much thought and consideration is therefore given to this process and the placement of the soldering points during the design and planning process.

A good designer-maker understands that skilled soldering is essential to the production of well-made pieces and a good preparation process is vital to successful soldering. Every designer possesses his or her own individual creative style and personal soldering methods. The following pages present and introduce a selection of interesting soldering and finishes that can be achieved.

MULTI-CULTURE RINGS
Felicity Peters

The main bead features on these three rings are constructed from corrugated formed sheet metal which has been shaped into various lengths of tube. Gently tapping the top and base of each piece depresses the tube into a flattened bead shape.

By hollowing a recess into the firebrick, each bead can sit securely in place to allow the soldering of the base and top disks. During the soldering of the top and base, air has been released via the spaces between the corrugations.

To solder the claws of the settings, drilled holes and wire were inserted and soldered in place. The rub-over setting was soldered directly onto the top disc. Finally, the beads were filed and fitted to the curve of the ring and the shanks soldered onto the bead. Hard silver solder was used for the joins on the bead so the shank was carefully connected with medium silver solder.

INDULGENCE HAND PIECE
Alexandra Tosto

Soldering tube onto the back of the flower creates a central location for the leaf shape. A drilled hole on the leaf connects the soldered tube, centrally positioning the flower before soldering occurs.

To secure the parts while soldering, the flower was placed upside down and the tube was held with reverse-action tweezers. Once these two parts were soldered, the back leaf was also held upside down and inserted into the tube before being joined. Finally, the claws of the setting were secured in place with medium silver solder, leaving the previous hard silver solder joins undisturbed.

TACTUS RING
Claudio Pino

The movement system of this wonderful piece works because of the combination of solder joins and hinges. This elaborate ring has been created from three metals: silver, copper, and brass, 95 components, and in excess of 100 solder joins. To allow movement between the sections of the ring, eight hinges have been applied. Hard, medium, and easy solders were all applied, and binding wire was used during the soldering stages. The combination of textures, shaped components, and various colored metals and stones, as well as the ingenious design, has produced this magnificent sculptural piece.

PIERCED RING NO. 5
Allyson Bone

The hand-pierced intricate pattern on the side of this ring has allowed the safe soldering of an otherwise enclosed space. After piercing, a flat sheet of silver was scored and folded to create the formed sides. Once the folded seams were soldered, a slightly larger top plate was soldered in place to allow solder to flow. Excess metal was then removed.

The bow detail was sweat soldered in place and then the top section of the ring was soldered to the shank, held in place with the assistance of honeycomb bricks and a 3rd hand soldering jig. Finishing the piece off with an intense black, oxidized finish gives this piece its striking, bold look.

GOLD ROSE NECKPIECE
Suzan Rezac

The combination of patinated Japanese metal alloy Shakudo with 18kt yellow gold produces a bold statement piece. By inlaying these two together, the contrast in color really stands out. To create this wonderful piece, a flat piece of Shakudo (black metal) was pierced and the 18kt yellow gold pieces then arduously inlaid. Once all the parts were perfectly fitted together, they were soldered in stages before being domed. This process was repeated to produce a second dome before the two were secured with binding wire and soldered together to create a perfect, hollow sphere. The stem of the piece has been produced from curved tube with sweat soldered thorns, which were pierced from silver sheet.

PINK CHAIN
Amy Logan

The use of wire does not have to be restricted to the production of fine or delicate pieces. By shaping, soldering, and coloring, this strong, bold, graphic neckpiece has been achieved.

Each individual link has been shaped and connected to fashion this chain. The joins between the wires and the connections were coated in borax flux and soldered with wire solder. Stick feeding the solder onto the joins allows quick, multiple soldering actions to be achieved. This technique is ideal for soldering a piece which has multiple joins, and for wire, which can be at high risk of melting from prolonged exposure to soldering heat.

SOUND & RHYTHM RING
Zehava Hashai-Spellman

This bold statement piece is fabricated using a soldering and slotting system, which allows parts to move and create noise.

By soldering quite simple shapes, the designer can create strong bold pieces of jewelry. However, irregular soldering work can be more visible on clean, simple forms.

The production of this ring involved three cones that were constructed and cut with slots to allow them to be inserted into one another. To ensure the pieces were positioned accurately, the two cones on either side were held together with stainless steel split pins and then soldered. Once secured with binding wire to the ring shank, the two cones were soldered.

The final cone was threaded through the two pre-soldered cones and two heavy stone set wires were applied to prevent this piece from coming out. Tight holes were drilled into the top cone and pre-set wire forced into the space to hold all the pieces securely in position. The stones were set before the final solder due to their inaccessible position and heat-resistant gel was applied to prevent heat damage to the stones. After cleaning with emery papers, the ring was finished with a satin matte effect.

BLACK HALO RING
Drew Perridge

The method of interlocking parts made from sheet silver has allowed the designer to fabricate a complicated and detailed ring. Finishing the piece with a jet black ruthenium enhances the brightness and color of the stones against this powerful background.

This complex piece has been made from three main components. The ring shank has been constructed from two large domes that have had their top sections cut away and have been soldered together along their edges to create a "V"-shaped platform. The central feature has been fabricated from pierced round disks, which were folded and cut with slots and inserted onto the ring shank. Once all the pieces were applied, the ring shank was held upside down and soldered from the back in one action. Soldering many parts simultaneously reduces the risks involved with multi-join soldering. The final stage was the soldering of the four tube settings. Cutting and slotting pieces together can assist in the soldering process. It allows pieces to be held securely and tightly together that otherwise would have been difficult to balance.

STRIKE 12 AND MAGIC DIES
Fiona McCulloch

The main cage structure that houses the clock in this magnificent piece was soldered by inserting wire into drilled holes on the top and base bezel sections. The wires were held in place with large sections of fire-proof sheet and were soldered in groups of three which were then coated in solder inhibitor while the next three were soldered. This cage construction was then slotted securely into the central etched cylinder.

The domed wheels and the central cylinder have soldered outer bezels and were attached together with two heavyweight curved square wires which were soldered in place.

To assist with the multiple solder joins in this piece, binding wire, jigs, solder inhibitors, and multiple melting point solders have be applied.

MIRRORED ELLIPSE PENDANT
Helen London

Filigree work adds intricate and delicate detailing to a piece of jewelry, but due to the fineness of wire employed and the numerous joins, the soldering of this type of feature can be complicated.

This pendant has been fabricated in two main sections. Each eclipse shape was created with an outer border frame which the filigree wire patterns were positioned into. Piece by piece, each individual wire was made to sit tightly in place, allowing its natural tension to spring and to hold it securely to the other pieces. This creates the closest fit and the most favorable soldering joins. Once all the pieces had been positioned, borax flux was coated over the entire surface area before powdered hard solder was sprinkled onto the surface. The excess powdered solder was brushed off prior to the application of heat from a handheld butane torch.

When both sections were soldered, they were shaped and formed into curves before being placing one on top of another. The points at the top and base were lined up and soldered with medium solder. The final solder joins were those at the top and base jump rings.

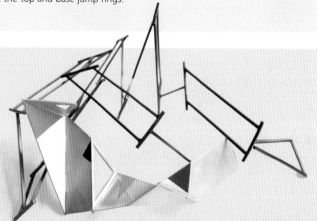

MULTIVARIABLE NECKLACE
Ruth Laird

This angular neckpiece was constructed from silver sheet, wire, and tubing. The chain was fabricated by butt soldering sections of square wire to pieces of tube which were then hinged together to form the connections. To create the center piece, silver sheet was scored, folded, and soldered before being partially hinged to additional wire and sheet shapes. Once the parts were securely connected, the piece was completed by oxidizing the chain and coating the cooked silver parts with spray paint. The combination of soldered and hinged parts allows flexibility and movement in this piece.

HONEYCOMB DREAM RING

Alexandra Tosto

The enamel-led feature of this ring has been constructed from four separately cast components. To solder the cast parts successfully, each was held upside down and secured with reverse action tweezers before stick feed soldering was carried out. This technique allows solder to flow into difficult-to-reach areas.

Once the top section of the ring was successfully soldered, the ring shank was held in place with reverse action tweezers and paillons of hard silver solder were placed on all points of contact between the top section and ring shank, and the two were soldered together. The enamel used is a cold version so this piece avoided being exposed to high kiln temperatures which would have affected the solder joins.

MINERAL COLLECTION OCTAGONAL PENDANT

Laura Moore Jewelry

Pieces that look simple can be the most complicated to fabricate and solder. This delicately formed 9kt gold wire pendant is an example of this. The gold wires were manipulated to meet perfectly before being soldered together. To create the internal octagonal shape, the end of a second piece of wire was formed into a "V" shape before being soldered to the inside of the original octagon. Once this join was soldered, the wire was manipulated and shaped to carry on to the next point of the outer octagon, which was also soldered. This process was repeated until the internal octagonal shape had been formed and soldered.

The sides were constructed from eight lengths of wire that were soldered to each corner of the outer octagonal shape. Two different melting point solders were used at this stage. Throughout the construction liquid flux was used as it works well with both gold and wire pieces.

MARGARET RING

Katherine Agnew

It is sensible to fabricate pieces of jewelry from as few elements as possible. If you are able to make a piece from two parts instead of four, then do so. This will create a stronger piece and limit the risk of parts becoming disengaged during the soldering of multiple joins.

This geometrically formed ring has been ingeniously created from one sheet of silver. The pattern, ring shank, and claw settings have been carefully pierced out before areas were scored and folded to create the cluster feature on the top of the ring shank.

To successfully solder, the shank of the ring was held in place with pieces of honeycomb brick, allowing the cluster feature to overhang. This allowed the maker to see and access all areas for the placement of solder and to distribute heat evenly.

Prior to soldering, flux was applied to the area and heated gently to allow the piece to become hot, then fluxed paillons of solder were applied to the joins. This ensured the solder stayed in place and was positioned exactly where required. Upon heat being applied, the solder flows, connecting the joins and securing the folded parts together. The partially oxidized finish gives the piece depth and allows the citrine to be a prominent feature.

LEST WE FORGET RING—KRAKOW 2009

Felicity Peters

This truly magnificent ring has been created from 51 silver and one 18kt gold cast chairs. Each chair has been carefully positioned before being soldered securely in place using only hard silver solder.

To create a secure setting for the first three chairs, three square holes were cut into the ring shank to hold one leg from each chair. Once these were soldered, between three and seven additional chairs were set up against the ring and also soldered in position. In order to secure further chairs in location, a 3rd hand jig was applied to hold the ring shank in place, while firebricks were positioned to support the parts during further soldering.

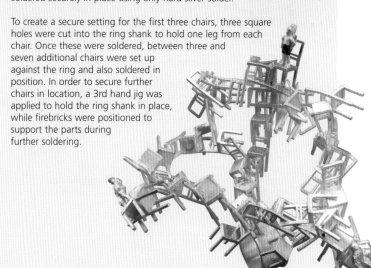

3 WOODLANDS RING

Lisa McGovern

This organically formed set of rings has been created by casting, fusing, and soldering. Using these three techniques has allowed the designer to create pieces with a really fluid and natural form.

The ring shanks have been created with wound square silver wire which has been fused with a central shank. The main element of each ring has been produced by lost wax, or water casting, and secured to the ring shanks with hard silver solder. To allow the cast pieces to solder successfully and prevent excess consumption of solder, just enough heat has been applied to allow solder to flow and join parts together.

To keep the finish in line with the organic look of the pieces, the rings have remained unpolished. The white matte finish is created by immersing the pieces in pickle solution and the dark areas have been oxidized.

PEARL BUBBLE EARRINGS

Melania Zucchi

The silver granulations not only give this pair of earrings a soft and tactile look but beautifully echo the shape, finish, and contrasting colors of the pearls.

To build the granules, a tapered setting was created with a soldered rounded base. Due to the spherical shape of the piece, the area worked on is tilted during soldering so it sits on a flat plane. To apply the granules, the piece was heated before a coat of liquid flux was administered with a pipette. Each granule was then heated and held next to a solder snippet to which it was affixed. This piece was positioned onto the fluxed area before another granule was applied. Once 4–5 granules were in place, the piece was heated to allow the solder to melt and flow. These soldered granules were then used to position and hold in place additional granules. Although time-consuming, the results of this procedure produce this beautiful "bubble-" like effect.

SEGMENT CLUSTER RING

Nicola Morrison

The linking up of the formed shapes in the top cluster gives this ring a really lovely tactile quality.

Construction began with two holes being drilled through the top section of the ring shank. A "U"-shaped piece of $\frac{1}{32}$ in (1mm) round wire was inserted into one of the holes until it was flush with the inside of the shank. After the soldering of this end of the wire with snippets of silver solder, the textured and shaped segments were threaded through the other end. After the insertion of the last segment, the free end of the wire was slotted into the second drilled hole and soldered closed, securing the segment cluster in place. As the segments sit very close together, a coating of heat-resistant gel was applied to prevent solder from running between the pieces and preventing their movement.

After soldering, the ring was carefully cleaned with a selection of wet and dry emery papers. The finished ring was then placed into a barrel polisher to finish the segment before the shank was hand polished on mops to give a highly polished finish.

CALYX II RING

Sophia Georgiopoulou

Although this ring gives the impression that it has been cast in one piece, it was in fact, fabricated from wire and sheet silver. The shank was constructed from heavyweight round wire and the cone from a pierced, drilled, and formed flat sheet that was soldered closed with hard silver solder. To ensure a tight fit, the base of the cone was cut and shaped to fit the curve of the ring shank and was held in place with binding wire, a 3rd hand jig, and reverse action tweezers while soldering.

Upon the successful soldering of cone to shank, granules were applied with the assistance of gum arabic or gum tragacanth. Once the glue had dried, a mixture of powdered solder and filed borax was scattered over the surface and the piece heated until the solder flow and the granules were secured in place. The piece was finished with an oxidized finish and a contrasting shocking pink enamel.

MERRY GO ROUND RING
Wing Mun Devenney

For the construction of this ring, air holes were drilled into the top of each bead to enable the release of air during soldering. These holes were discreetly covered with the settings and stones. The rotating movement of the central "three-dome" section was achieved by threading the central soldered tube onto a central bar before carefully soldering on a larger silver bead to secure the piece. Solder inhibitor was applied to the central bar and the tube to avoid the two from soldering together, thus preventing the rotating action.

Further solder joins were applied for the granulation details and the suspended beads, as well as the spinning piece and the double ring shank. To deal with the multiple solder joins on this piece, multiple grades of solder were used and the assistance of solder inhibitors and soldering jigs were employed.

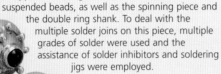

A FOREST
Dauvit Alexander

This truly magnificent piece has been painstakingly constructed and built from various metal types, including brass, copper, nickel, gold, pure iron, and silver.

Although this piece is elaborate and complicated, much time was spent planning the construction to ensure its successful completion. Much of the intricate pierced detailing was created on CAD (computer assisted design) and then hand pierced before being built into box-type constructions.

Although the majority of the solder work was comprised in the center piece, the chain required joining too. Each cast component was linked with jump rings and soldered closed.

There are extensive soldering techniques and mixed-metal joins involved, including sweat soldering, butt soldering, the soldering of silver to gold, iron to silver, gold to nickel, gold to copper, and silver to copper. To allow the successful joining of iron, the designer has used silver as an intermediate metal between the layers.

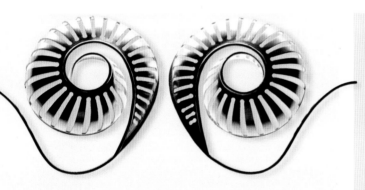

VOLUTE LARGE SPIRAL EARRINGS
Cara Tonkin

To create this formed pair of earrings, the spiral shapes were machine-water cut before being raised into their structures. To ensure the silver wire along the edges was soldered successfully, the process was undertaken in stages, section by section. Binding the start of the wire to the piece provided security while soldering occurred. Once the first section was secured, the wire was formed further around the piece and again secured with binding wire and soldered. This process was continued until the wire was soldered successfully in place around the whole piece.

LITTLE BLACK PRECIOUSNESS
Filipa Oliveira

To solder the components and settings onto this round shank, a steel ring was applied as a soldering jig. By placing and positioning a few parts at a time on the curve of the steel ring, soldering could more easily be achieved. Once a section was soldered, a few more components were positioned and soldered. This process was repeated until the ring was complete. The intricate and delicate filigree detailing within some of the framed components was soldered flat against a honeycomb brick with spray flux and powdered solder, both of which prevent excess movement of the parts.

CIRCLE FRILL BROOCH
Leila Swift

The intricate pierced detail along with the soft matte white finish gives a beautiful, lace-like quality to this brooch. The decorative detailing on the flat face and the internal ring has been hand pierced before the ring was formed and soldered. During the soldering of the frame to the upper side, binding wire was applied to maintain the shape and keep the frame securely closed. Once these two parts were successfully soldered, the additional hand-pierced ornamental feature was leveled at an angle against the piece and held in position with steel pins. Easy solder was applied to reduce the risk of previous solder joins from re-flowing. The final solder joins for the brooch fittings were also carried out with easy silver solder.

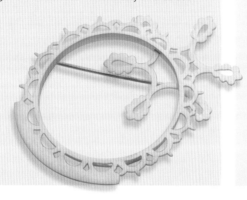

SPIRAL BROOCH
Kayo Saito

To achieve the numerous solder joins oriented in an upright position, each piece of partially planished wire was spot welded into place. By welding the parts, the designer is able to position the pieces at the desired angles and secure them while soldering takes place in one action. Instead of the painstaking and risky procedure of multiple soldering joins, this technique allows many parts to be soldered together. In order to prevent the wires from melting, the piece was elevated off the firebrick and heat was applied from below. Hard solder was applied for the wire details and medium solder for the brooch fitting to reduce the risk of previous joins moving.

STRIPED NECKLACE
Robert Feather

The mixing of colored golds instantly adds character to a piece; additionally, the rose gold in this neckpiece ties in well with the warm golden tones of the citrine. The top part of this piece was created by soldering white, rose, and green gold sections onto a yellow gold back sheet. To achieve the flush surface across the colored sections, the piece was rolled and shaped before being soldered to an edged frame. The stone setting and square wire detail were applied and soldered last of all.

PAPER SILVER PRINT RING
Frieda Lühl

Gold and silver make an interesting contrast and by adding a black oxidized finish the color of the gold is enhanced further. Additionally, the gold wire detail mirrors the golden hairline characteristics in the central rutilated quartz stone. The combination of these features marry well together.

The construction of this ring started with roll-printed fine silver which was pierced into an oval shape and domed slightly to give it more form. A frame was then soldered around this piece before the rub-over setting was applied and soldered to the center. The 18kt fine gold wire has been shaped and fitted against the domed surface and soldered with medium silver solder.

Once the top section of the ring was completed, a soldered ring shank was filed to fit this center piece. The shank was then soldered to the central part using medium silver solder.

Upon completion of soldering, the piece was cleaned and polished before the stone was set and the oval section oxidized.

INCREMENTI BROOCH
Sophia Georgiopoulou

The intricate spherical embellishments on this brooch marry together well with the bold solid pearls and the rich sparkle from the faceted stones. Building and soldering onto an open frame gives the piece a more delicate appearance.

The frame has been constructed from thick solid gold wire with a soldered piece of tube to house the brooch pin. Numerous pierced domes were soldered together to fashion spherical forms before granules were applied. Further half domes were soldered with claw settings and petal details with the assistance of binding wire and reverse-action tweezers. Third hand jigs were employed to assist in the positioning of the spheres and half domes along the frame for soldering. Once all the pieces were soldered, granules were positioned and soldered onto the front and back of the brooch. The piece was then finished and the stones set.

TROUBLE WITH LICHEN
Dauvit Alexander

It is common to produce pieces of jewelry using a combination of joining techniques. These can vary from soldering parts together to securing a stone in place with a stone setting. In the case of this ring, parts have been soldered along with stone settings and the insertion of components. This ring illustrates how a piece can be constructed and joined by using not only soldering but a mixture of fixtures to allow the successful joining of components.

This piece combines the use of non-precious and precious metals, iron, and silver. The internal iron shank is joined to an external silver band before the stone settings, protruding rod holders, and granulations have been soldered. To position and solder the granules securely in place, a mixture of easy silver solder paste and gum arabic was applied.

The three elongated iron rods were inserted into the tight-fitting holders and secured in place with silver folds. The stones were set and the whole piece oxidized to finish the ring.

CHALICE CUFFLINKS
Suzanne Potter

By threading wire through the center of the components, this pair of cufflinks was aligned and secured for soldering. Using a longer length of wire, the upper large flower details were soldered before the domes and cones were attached. The length of wire is cut, and the small flower threaded and secured with a soldered granule on the tip of the wire. The final soldering action is between the edge of the dome and the round rim. Once complete, this piece has been highly polished and oxidized internally on the dome and cone, which are both areas that would otherwise have been difficult to access. The oxidized interiors provide a strong contrast to the polished flower parts, resulting in a bold, graphic aesthetic.

SPACE DOME RING
Wing Mun Devenney

Soldering of parts at angles can prove difficult, but using soldering jigs and working out ways that parts can be inserted into each other can assist greatly. In the construction of this piece, a section of tube was soldered to the center of the inside of the top dome. Then a hole was drilled in the center of the lower dome and the dome was threaded through the tube. By inserting the end of the tube into a drilled hole on the top side of the shank and with further assistance of a 3rd hand jig, the pieces were secured during soldering. Hard and easy solder were applied to solder together the parts of this free-standing ring.

Chapter 1
Getting Started In Soldering

Soldering is a process that can be carried out successfully only when all equipment, materials, steps, and procedures have been understood. A basic selection of tools will offer the jeweler numerous production options; as the jeweler's ability advances, so can their range of equipment. Investing in good-quality tools will ensure longevity and accuracy. If advice is required from an expert, then obtain it before proceeding with use. Check if tools require oil on a regular basis or if they have to be cleaned and polished.

This chapter is an introduction to soldering, covering all the fundamentals and key issues that need to be considered prior to getting started. Here you will learn the essential "ingredients" of soldering: beginning with choosing tools, metals, and solders and moving on to vital pre-soldering procedures. With the experience gained from this chapter, a jeweler can begin to construct and solder confidently and successfully.

Torches

A blow torch blasts either air or oxygen mixed with a combustible gas. When this combination is ignited, it produces sufficient heat for jewelry work such as annealing and soldering.

The key function of a soldering torch is to project the ideal flame to heat the soldering area to the right temperature to allow the solder to flow successfully. To prepare for soldering you must understand the torch and the type of flame to apply. There are a number of torches available and the choice can either be a personal preference or a technical requirement. Here we take a look at the broad range of torches on the market: from those that are affordable and ideal for the home solderer right up to the costly and less commonly used specialty torches.

Hand torch

Atmospheric torch

Portable Hand Torches
BEGINNER
How does it work?
The size of the flame is adjusted with an easy-to-operate switch. Hand torches are available with butane or propane gas and can be bought from jewelry equipment suppliers or from hardware or cookware stores. Hand-held torches are suitable for silver, and 9kt and 18kt gold.

Strengths These types of torch are ideal for beginner jewelers as they are compact and easy to handle. They can be held and controlled with one hand, freeing the other to maneuver tweezers, parts, or solder.

Weaknesses The gases are simple to refill but quickly consumed, making this type of torch expensive and often bothersome to run. In addition, due to the size of flame, only small, basic soldering jobs can be achieved. Ideally, once a jeweler develops their soldering skills, a more advanced torch system should be adopted.

Atmospheric Torches
INTERMEDIATE
How does it work?
Atmospheric torches are commonly used by independent jewelers. They function on pressurized canisters of propane, butane, or acetylene gases, and draw oxygen from the air.

To turn the torch on, the gas valve is opened, allowing the gas to hiss out. This is then ignited with a friction lighter. You must ensure the rubber hoses are hole-free and attached securely, and that the canisters are on a flat surface and unlikely to be knocked over or jostled.

The methods for increasing the heat are to increase the gas, allowing the flame to be larger; changing the nozzle size; or bringing the flame closer to your work, so that the hottest part of the flame will be in closer contact with the area you wish to heat. Alternatively, you can add a regulator to the gas canister to control the amount of gas or air.

Jewelry suppliers and plumbing and hardware stores keep these torches in stock.

Strengths This is a self-regulating system that mixes the gas and air in equal quantities. It is therefore easier to use than most torches as it only has one control to adjust.

Weaknesses The amount of air drawn in to the torch cannot be controlled separately, but adjusting the gas knob allows more or less air intake through holes on the nozzle area. Because air is nearly 80 percent nitrogen, much less oxygen is supplied to these torches than those that have a separate air or oxygen supply, so the heat produced can be less intense.

Gas and Air/Oxygen Torches
INTERMEDIATE
How does it work?
Gas and air/oxygen torches work with a combination of gas and a separate oxygen or pressurized

air supply, which are connected from canisters or the mains with rubber hose pipes. These torches can be run on propane, butane, or acetylene. Pure oxygen is highly flammable when mixed with other gases or compounds, so compressed air is more commonly used. To switch the torch on, the gas mechanism is released and the pilot flame is ignited with a friction burner. The size and power of the flame is controlled by adjusting the air and gas knobs.

Strengths The size and power of the flame can be adjusted, giving more control. These are often used for casting or welding metal.

Weaknesses It can take time to master the two controls: the gas and the air. Furthermore, due to the highly flammable nature of oxygen, it can be difficult to get insurance for home use.

Bench-Secured Swivel Action Torches
INTERMEDIATE–ADVANCED
How does it work?
This piece of equipment (also known as a Birmingham Sidelight) is not commonly used by jewelers today, and is not easy to obtain. It is attached to a workbench and works with a gas flame ignited from a horizontal brass tube. This main body has a swivel mechanism and, when moved toward the soldering area, the flame accentuates; when moved back, the flame reduces. During

soldering or annealing work, the flame is manipulated into an intense and more focused heat by the operator blowing air through tapered copper or brass tubing. The jeweler holds the end of the tube in their mouth with their teeth.

Strengths This type of soldering equipment allows the operator to have both hands free and, as the jeweler powers the flame, they therefore have much more control.

Weaknesses It produces a relatively small flame that is sufficient for a majority of jewelry work but is neither hot enough nor large enough for larger metal-smith items or metals that require higher temperatures. It is not widely used and for this reason could be difficult to source.

Mouth-Blown Torches
INTERMEDIATE–ADVANCED
How does it work?
This handheld torch is also not commonly used. It has two

pipes, one supplying gas and the other air. The difference is that the air is produced by the jeweler blowing into the secondary pipe.

Strengths The release of air is produced by the user so there can be greater control of the flame than with some other torches. The user can easily adjust the flame by controlling their exhalation without having to use their hands, thus keeping them free.

Weaknesses Plenty of practice is required to achieve the even and regular exhaling of air. Irregular breaths create a sporadic flame that is insufficient for heating or soldering. As with the bench-secured swivel action torch, this equipment is not widely used and is not suitable for larger items or high-temperature metals.

Micro Soldering Systems
INTERMEDIATE–ADVANCED
How does it work?
Micro Soldering Systems are also commonly known as oxy hydrogen torches. They produce their own oxygen and hydrogen from the water supply.

Strengths The flame produced is precise and intensely hot, making a micro soldering system extremely useful for soldering high-melting-temperature metals such as platinum and palladium. The join produced has very little discoloration. The advantage of using these torches is that they do not require replacement gas and air cylinders. Once the system is set up there should be minimal cost, but you will need to buy chemicals that are only available from the manufacturers.

Weaknesses The small flame makes them impractical for larger pieces of work.

Micro Soldering System

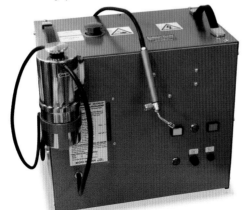

Portable Gas and Oxygen torch

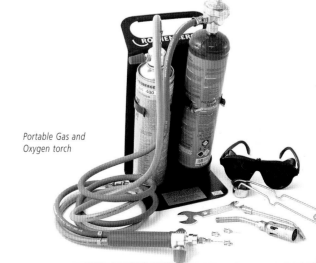

Laser Welders

ADVANCED

How does it work?

Laser welders are boxlike constructions in which the work is placed through a confined area. The parts for joining are viewed through a microscope, which allows very precise work. A foot pedal is used to control the laser projection, and the size, depth, and numbers of laser shots are all adjustable.

They work by emitting a laser onto the join, which melts the surrounding area and fuses the two metals together. No solder is necessary, and the join achieved is invisible and strong.

Strengths They can be used to weld precious and some non-precious metals together. As the heat is focused on a localized area, multi-join pieces can be fabricated without the risk of other joins opening and the piece collapsing. This also makes these welders effective for jewelry repairs in areas that are close to heat-sensitive materials such as gemstones or enamels. They are also helpful for tacking pieces together prior to soldering, thus avoiding the more complicated set-up stages and making the soldering process quicker and the fabrication possibilities expansive.

Weaknesses For silver pieces, this type of equipment does have a tendency to melt the join area and make the metal splatter. To prevent the reflective properties of silver from creating a weak join, the area for welding can be covered with marker pen.

For a note on the strength of the join and the cost of this type of equipment, see "PUK Welders" at right.

PUK Welders

ADVANCED

How does it work?

PUK welders are micro versions of the TIG (tungsten inert gas) welders that are commonly used in engineering environments. The PUK has been specially designed for jewelry and works by forming an arc between a . tungsten electrode and the piece for joining. This action is performed within an inert gas atmosphere, and the heat created fuses the join together.

Strengths Similar to the laser welder, adjusting the heat input can control the thickness and size of join.

A PUK welder carries out similar tasks to those a laser welder can achieve, but the cost of a PUK is much lower. The benefit of the PUK and laser welders is achieving almost any type of join that may have been impossible with soldering. However, the possibilities with these types of equipment are extensive, and understanding and applying new technology is of great benefit. To test them out, try your local colleges or art schools.

Weaknesses The laser and PUK welders produce joins that are weaker than traditional solder joins, as they create multiple weld spots rather than one secure solder join. For an independent jeweler, the cost of these welders may not be financially viable.

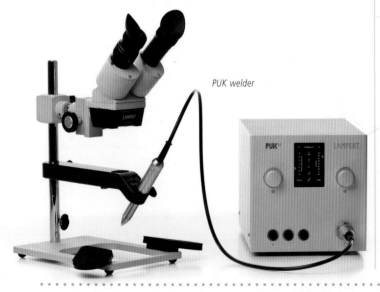

PUK welder

Gases

Propane allows the flame to burn carbon-free and clean. The flame is extremely hot and bright white. Propane burns hotter than butane so can be more suitable for high-melting-temperature solders. The gas canisters are easily attainable from camping equipment stores. This gas is often preferred for outdoor use as it does not freeze easily.

Butane is probably the most commonly purchased gas for jewelry soldering. It burns cleaner and has less toxicity than propane, so it is safer to use indoors—but always check with your insurnce company. The physical properties of propane and butane are similar and there is no significant temperature difference. Compared to propane, butane gas produces more energy, so it is longer lasting and more cost-effective.

Acetylene torches produce the hottest flame, but they do not burn clean, leaving carbon deposits. To avoid this, oxygen has to be added during the ignition of the torch, but due to safety considerations, most jewelry torches use air instead of oxygen. An acetylene torch is often used for high-melting-temperature metals such as platinum (which is unaffected by an unclean carbon flame) and palladium, or for larger metal work.

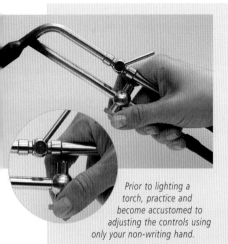

Prior to lighting a torch, practice and become accustomed to adjusting the controls using only your non-writing hand.

Handling a Flame

The jeweler should learn to hold and master the torch with their non-writing hand. This will leave the stronger and more commanding hand free to control and move parts, as well as apply solder when necessary, often during the heating process. It also allows the application of parts to solder points at the precise moment of solder flow, stops parts from overheating, and prevents exhausting the flux.

Order to Use Flames

The ideal flame is blue, not too sharp in shape, and quiet. If it is too bushy, the flame will not offer precise or sufficient heat. If it is too noisy and sharp, this oxidizing flame will prevent solder from flowing. I find the following method works best, but other jewelers set the flame to neutral throughout the soldering process.

1. Turn the torch to a bushy reducing flame to heat the parts gently in order to prevent the solder from blowing off and to allow the flux to expand. This flame can also be applied to heat the parts prior to placing fluxed solder to a difficult-to-solder area. The fluxed solder will adhere and stay positioned at the exact spot.

2. Then adjust the flame to a more controlled blue neutral flame to progress with the soldering process.

Moving the Flame

To achieve even heat distribution and allow solder to flow, the flame of the torch should be moving at all times. Furthermore, to direct flowing solder along a seam, the flame must be moved along to maintain sufficient heat for the solder to flow.

1. Circular movements
2. Zigzagging across surfaces
3. Pointing and directing flame to base part/s
4. Moving flame along a solder seam

Types of Flames

The jeweler must distinguish the differences between flame types and learn how to adjust the torch to achieve the optimum flame necessary for the work they wish to carry out. Please note that the oxidizing and reducing flames can only be achieved with a torch that has adjustable controls for the air and gases. Portable hand torches and atmospheric torches are not adjustable and will only produce neutral flames.

1. Oxidizing flame

This is made from more oxygen than gas and will cause excess oxidization to the surface of the metal, preventing solder from flowing.

Appearance and sound This flame is recognized by its pale color and a high-pitched, sharp hissing sound.

2. Neutral flame

Equal parts gas and oxygen and the ideal flame for soldering as it decreases the level of oxidization. Portable hand torches and atmospheric torches will produce only this type of flame.

Appearance and sound Blue, with a slight yellow tip, and soft and bushy; this flame is the least noisy. The hottest area of this flame is at the end of the inner cone. Once flux has started to dry and there is no risk of movement in the pieces, the hottest part is applied to bring the metal to the desired temperature for solder to flow.

3. Reducing flame

Also known as carburizing, contains more gas than oxygen.

Appearance and sound
Bushy and rather jagged-looking; front of the flame is orangey red; quite loud.
Although this flame is hot enough to solder and can reduce the amount of oxides on the solder surface, the larger, less localized flame is not as precise as a neutral flame. Ideal for annealing and for heating the parts prior to adjusting to a neutral flame for soldering. The front of the flame emits less heat and can be used for that purpose.

1

Oxidizing flame

2

Neutral flame

3

Reducing flame

Other Tools

The jeweler's selection of tools and equipment is essential to the construction and soldering processes. Every tool has its own unique function and, when applied correctly, can assist in many procedures.

1. Revolving turntable

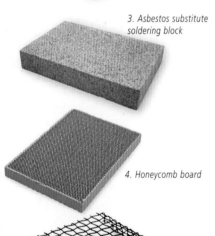

2. Charcoal brick

3. Asbestos substitute soldering block

4. Honeycomb board

5. Stainless steel mesh

Revolving Turntable (1)

The revolving turntable is a good base for a soldering station. It is a strong and heavy stand with a revolving platform to house soldering bricks and boards. The turntable feature allows the jeweler to access and view all sides of the piece, and allows heat distribution to all 360 degrees. Turntables are available in various sizes, with a cast-iron or aluminum base, and a ceramic table-top surface. Place fireproof bricks or board to reflect any heat and to protect the background of the soldering station from fire. Do not solder directly onto the turntable unless it has a ceramic top.

Heat-Proof Blocks and Bricks

Heat-proof surfaces not only protect the soldering area but also reflect heat back onto the parts for soldering. There are many types of bricks and blocks available, each with their own unique characteristics.

Charcoal bricks (2) both hold and reflect heat. This type of brick also creates a reducing atmosphere, with less oxygen, which creates a cleaner soldering surrounding and helps the solder to melt faster, as well as preventing build-up of fire-stain. Due to the softness of the charcoal, pins to position and hold pieces in place can be applied directly into the brick. Pieces can also be broken off to position parts or prop items, or the bricks can be carved into when positioning awkwardly shaped pieces.

Charcoal retains heat, so it is best to spray these bricks with water after soldering to prevent damage to the bricks and a fire hazard. Charcoal also has a tendency to split when heated, so the piece should be bound with binding wire or protected by a metal casing. Charcoal should only be used in a well-ventilated area.

Asbestos substitute soldering blocks (3) are normally available in small sizes and have quite a smooth, flat surface. They retain their shape and flat surface quite well, and are particularly durable when used at high heats.

Soldering sheets are large, flat sheets made from asbestos substitute. They can be positioned on top of the turntable, so soldering can be carried out directly; as a background prior to placing firebricks or blocks on top; or as a heat-proof background for your soldering area surface.

Magnesia soldering blocks are available in brick form. They are lightweight and soft enough to allow pinning into, carving into, and using sawed or broken-off sections to elevate parts for soldering.

Honeycomb board (4) is long-lasting and reflects heat well. Its holes can be used for placing pins and clips, as well as binding wire for creating unique holders for soldering difficult constructions. It is made from lightweight ceramics and has high-temperature resistance, so it is ideal for soldering high-melting-temperature metals.

Ceramic soldering blocks can resist intense heat, making them ideal for working with metals such as platinum.

Enamel stainless steel mesh sheet (5) is cut and shaped into wire supports for pieces of

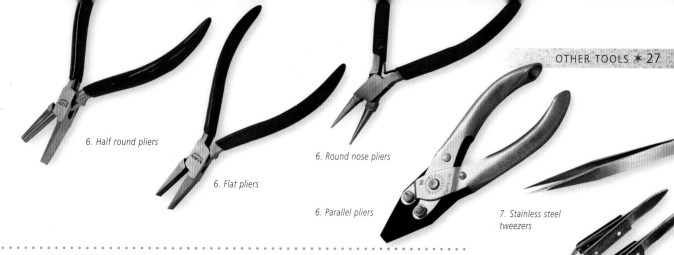

6. *Half round pliers*

6. *Flat pliers*

6. *Round nose pliers*

6. *Parallel pliers*

7. *Stainless steel tweezers*

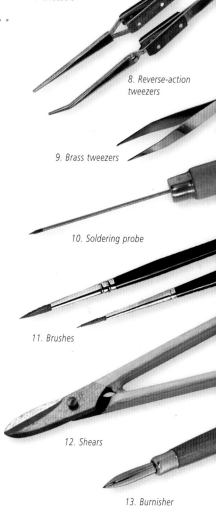

8. *Reverse-action tweezers*

9. *Brass tweezers*

10. *Soldering probe*

11. *Brushes*

12. *Shears*

13. *Burnisher*

enameling placed into kilns. However, the same supports or adapted forms can be used for placing pieces onto for soldering, and are especially useful for parts that need to be heated from below. The ideal set-up is to build a bridge-like system whereby two heatproof bricks are placed apart with the mesh sheet bridging the two. The parts for soldering are placed on the mesh bridge and heat is applied from below.

Soldering and Jewelry Production Tools

A selection of pliers (6) can be used for bending and shaping the metal prior to soldering and can also be useful for applying binding wire.

Stainless steel tweezers (7) are incredibly useful for jewelry soldering. They are used to transport and position solder and pieces. The ends must be kept as sharp and straight as possible. A good-quality pair will have precise, sharp ends that are able to pick up even the smallest piece of solder; lower-cost options are not suitable for fine jewelry work.

Reverse-action tweezers (8) are available in straight and curved, non-wooden- and wooden-handled versions. All of them are useful for holding in place an item for soldering, either balanced against a secure prop or held in position by the user. Caution should be applied when used for soldering to ensure that overheating does not occur, which could cause melting of the metal, or misshapes or marks on the piece. Reverse-action tweezers can be useful as they have a locking system to secure the piece and balance it into the desired position.

Brass tweezers or tongs (9) are used for placing and removing items from the pickle solution. Steel contaminates the pickle, so tweezers and binding wire should never be in contact.

Soldering picks or probes (10) are employed to move and direct solder. In addition, some jewelers heat solder paillons into granulated balls which are attached to the pick with assistance from flux, then placed into an exact position. This method is used for precision

application or where only minute amounts of solder are required.

Brushes (11) are not only used to apply flux but sometimes to help pick up and place solder. Having a selection of brushes will prove useful for other substances and chemicals that may be used during soldering. Flux brushes are available from specialty jewelry tool suppliers, but standard artist's brushes work just as well. Always use separate brushes for different fluxes and chemicals to avoid contamination.

Shears (12) are suitable for cutting thin metal sheet or wire, and for cutting solder. A reliable pair of shears, which is oiled and sharp, is essential to cutting accurately. Solder cutting pliers are also available and can offer a more accurate and uniform paillon size.

A burnisher (13) is used to rub and smooth. It can be useful for smoothing and covering porous areas of cast parts or for making a palladium or platinum solder join less noticeable.

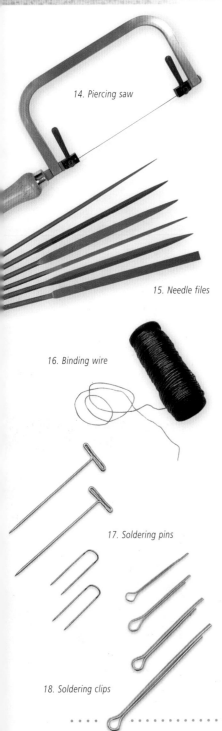

14. Piercing saw

15. Needle files

16. Binding wire

17. Soldering pins

18. Soldering clips

A piercing saw (14) and selection of blades are used for cutting parts. Use a good-quality saw and purchase finer blades for detailed work. Although it takes a little longer, the finer blade will ensure accuracy, in particular for inlaying or fitting pieces together.

Large and small needle files (15) are used for piercing, filing, and fitting. A good-quality selection will enable you to fit pieces together accurately so solder flows successfully. Files are also essential during cleaning for removing excess solder, scratches, and marks. A range of different shaped files will be able to fit into all types of gaps and small areas.

Torch lighters and holders must be chosen with safety in mind. The safest lighter options are friction lighters. Disposable gas-filled lighters can easily ignite or explode near a naked flame. If you choose to use matches, place them away from the torch when not in use. Torch holders allow safe and convenient positioning of the torch when switched off.

A ceramic or glass bowl filled with cool water should be placed near the soldering area to allow hot pieces to be immersed for cooling prior to being placed in pickle solution.

Soldering Jigs
It is essential to position and stabilize the pieces during soldering. Any movement can cause incorrect positioning or the piece to collapse. To avoid these problems, various types of equipment and tools are available. Bear in mind that any alien component attached to your soldering piece will draw heat away—this is called a heat sink. This can actually help to prevent excess heat in a particular area, but be careful not to position a heat sink in an area where heat is required.

3rd and 4th hands on bases are available with options of one or two arms and with and without tweezers. The version without tweezers allows the user to connect their own tweezers. The 4th hand option is available with a magnifying glass.

Binding wire (16) can be used to bind two or more pieces together to avoid movement or to prevent expansion and opening of seams. Always apply small kinks with round-nose pliers to allow flexibility and movement in the metal during the heating process, as this will prevent the wire marking the piece. Remember to remove all binding wire before placing a soldered piece into pickle solution. The steel wire will contaminate the pickle and any piece that is immersed.

Soldering wigs are made of a round disc of iron mesh, with a handle. They are ideal for soldering parts that require heat from below or above. When pieces are soldered on this wire mesh, less heat is drawn away from the parts, making the solder flow quicker.

Ceramic ring holders are used to hold rings or bezels in place during soldering. They allow the ring to be positioned at all types of angles, so pieces can be soldered onto any plane.

Soldering pins (17) could be virtually any **stainless steel pins**, such as jewelry merchandizing or dress-making pins. Just ensure that whatever pin you use is stainless steel and will withstand the heat. It is best to test pins against a torch flame before setting up.

Soldering clips (18) are useful for holding parts together. They can be made from the wire of a steel coat hanger, adapted from steel straps used in packing, cotter pins, or piano wire. By experimenting, you will find what works best for you. It is best to test against a torch flame before setting up.

Solder trays and grain assist with the positioning of awkwardly shaped or small, difficult-to-hold items. The silicon carbide grains are an ideal surface on which to position pieces, either by placing on top or partially imbedded.

Measuring Tools
A scribe (19) is used for marking onto metal, be it a midpoint or to draw a design

19. Scribe

20. Steel ruler

21. Engineer square

directly onto the piece. It can be used freehand or against a straight measuring tool such as a ruler or set square.

A steel ruler (20) is a must in measuring and is used as a guide to mark against. In a jeweler's workshop, only a metal ruler should be used, as a plastic version will not offer the accuracy or durability required.

An engineer or machinist square (21) is essential as a guide for measuring and marking, especially for right angles. Square or rectangular pieces can be placed on the thicker base to check for accuracy: Any light passing through will indicate your piece has not been trued to a right angle.

Pickle Solution (22)

Pieces that have been annealed, cast, or soldered will have oxides, investment plaster, flux, and fire-stains. To remove these surface marks, the pieces have to be immersed in pickle solution, which is usually a mixture of diluted acid and water. The most commonly used acid is sulfuric, which is available in powder or liquid form and then mixed with water. As this type of solvent is highly hazardous, you must consult the manufacturer's instructions prior to mixing and use. Every care should be taken to avoid contact with skin and clothing. Safety pickle solutions are also available. These work on the same principle as acid-based solutions but do not cause damage to skin or clothing.

Virtually all pickle solutions work best when warmed, so they should be placed in a ceramic container that can be immersed in warm water. The best option is to use a slow cooker, which not only keeps the solution warm but has a lid for safety. To place and remove items from the pickle solution without contaminating it, use only brass or plastic tweezers and tongs. Steel should never be placed in the pickle solution as it will leave a copper residue that will coat silver. After pickling, pieces must be washed thoroughly with water to remove all traces of acid to prevent erosion of the metal and solder.

Cleaning Equipment
Metal and wire brushes (23) are used for removing any excess flux and solder marks. A selection of jewelry brushes is also useful, with both soft and hard bristles and brass wire, available in various sizes. Brushes are best used under running water and with detergent when removing polish or dirt from your pieces.

Abrasive papers (24) are used in a sanding motion to remove solder, solder marks, file marks, scratches, and fire-stain. To achieve a good finish, start with a coarser level and work up to a finer grade. Grades are available between 150 and 2000, and in wet and dry options. Wet options are applied with water

and are ideal for use on large surface areas or on materials that may expel harmful dust particles. The benefit of using abrasive paper is the flexibility of cutting it to any size and folding it into different shapes and thicknesses.

Emery sticks (25) are available in various shapes and sizes to fit around the form of the piece you are cleaning. Wrapped in varying grades of emery paper, they can be easier to hold and apply pressure with than pieces of folded emery paper. Although these are readily available to purchase, they are easy and inexpensive to make from a variety of shaped wooden dowels and double-sided tape.

Water of Ayr stone is a wonderful tool for removing fire-stain but difficult to find. However, there are substitutes, such as Shah stone, on the market. Dip the stone into water before using against the metal in a circular motion.

Polishing compounds (26) can be used with standard polishing mops or on small detachable mops for hand-held devices. Some jewelers have limited space and choose to use hand-held polishing motors rather than the larger options.

Polishing cloths (27) are impregnated with polishing compounds suitable for various metals, be it silver, gold, or platinum group metals.

22. Pickle powder

23. Jewelry brushes

23. Brass wire brush

24. Abrasive papers

25. Emery sticks

27. Polishing cloths

26. Polishing compounds

Copper

Choosing a Metal

When designing a piece, it is important to carefully choose the metal you are going to use based on aesthetics, availability, weight, cost implications, as well as how easy it is to work with and what finishes are possible.

Take some time to plan the piece and determine the sizes and number of parts required; this will establish the amount of metal and materials necessary and ultimately the cost of the piece. Metals are grouped into ferrous (iron-based) and non-ferrous (further broken down into precious metals and base metals) types and there are many which are especially suited to jewelry production. Precious metals (such as gold, silver, platinum, and palladium) are so called due to their rarity; base metals on the other hand (such as copper, brass, and stainless steel) are more readily available and plentiful, making them less valuable. Presented here are a list of commonly used metals for the fabrication and soldering of jewelry. Platinum and palladium are valuable and more rarely used precious metals which require a high heat for soldering. They are discussed separately on pages 32–33.

Non-Ferrous: Precious Metals

Precious metals are available to purchase from bullion companies or specialty jewelry suppliers in a variety of forms and types. The price of precious metals fluctuates in the marketplace and can be dictated by the global supply and demand activity; therefore a sheet of metal ordered one day may differ in price the following day. When costing a piece for selling purposes, bear this in mind and factor in an average metal cost. Silver and gold are both highly malleable, allowing the shaping and forming of jewelry and accessories, and good conductors of heat, making them perfect for soldering. When cleaned and polished, these metals have beautiful reflective qualities.

Silver
Fine silver (which is 99.9% silver) is alloyed with copper to produce Britannia Silver or Sterling silver. Sterling silver which is also known as standard silver is 92.50% silver and 7.50% copper and Britannia Silver contains 95.80% silver and 4.20% copper.

Usage Fine silver is much too soft to produce entire pieces of jewelry; however it is used for intricate work such as weaving of fine wire or for enamel work. Britannia silver is ideal for production of larger, raised, or spun objects. Sterling silver is the most commonly used silver. Due to its softness, silver is not used in the setting of precious gemstones where platinum or

white gold are most suitable. Therefore it is usually used for dress, not high-end jewelry. Manageable cost makes it ideal for the creating of larger items.

Strengths Beautiful white luster. Malleable, reflective qualities and reasonable cost make it perfect for jewelry and accessories. Can be used for the setting of very delicate stones which may become damaged with less malleable metals.

Weaknesses Likely to become fire-stained during annealing and soldering. The can be removed but is time-consuming. Unworn silver jewelry becomes oxidized as it reacts with sulphur in the air which can result in a tarnished and black surface. Tarnish can be removed with a silver polishing cloth or silver cleaning solution.

Soldering Easily achievable with minimal equipment required.

Buying Readily available in many forms and shapes from jewelry suppliers. Silver is the most affordable precious metal.

Gold
A warm golden-colored metal with strong malleable qualities—ideal for jewelry making.

Usage 18kt gold, which is strong and rich in color, is the most popular in Western countries. 22kt gold is favored in many Asian countries with lesser karats seen as unvaluable.

Silver

The strength of white gold makes it ideal for gemstone setting. When using higher priced metals, great care should be taken to avoid excess waste of metal. Scraps and sweepings should be collected for recycling and refining purposes: melted, reshaped, and reused in a personal workshop or sold to a bullion dealer.

Strengths Malleable and strong so can be thinned to delicate proportions to form detailed and intricate pieces.

Weaknesses 24kt gold is very soft and rarely used for jewelry making. Gold can be prohibitively expensive, especially for large pieces, so consider your budget and the size of the piece. Mixing with a lower cost metal such as silver will curtail the cost. White gold cannot achieve the brilliant white appearance of platinum and palladium due to the alloys used. It is often plated with rhodium or platinum to achieve a whiter finish.

Soldering Each karat and color requires a matching solder to ensure corresponding melting temperatures and good color match. Borax cone flux will work effectively but the use of liquid flux can often be a benefit, especially for fine detailed work. Gold solders require higher temperatures to melt than that of silver; however the same torches and equipment applied in silver solder can also be used for gold.

Buying Karats (24kt, 22kt, 18kt, 14kt, 9kt) denote the amount of pure gold contained. The higher the karat, the greater the gold content, the deeper the color, the higher the cost. Available in a variety of colors, the most common are yellow, rose, white, and green.

Non-Ferrous: Base Metals
With the increasing prices of precious metals, base metals have become more popular in jewelry making. A combination of precious and nonprecious can also be used and is often more appealing.

Copper
Copper is a warm rose pink metal which is attractive for jewelry making and soldering.

Usage Often used by beginner jewelers and solderers. Low cost and availability make it ideal for experimenting with. Often combined with silver to create color contrast.

Strengths Highly malleable, good conductor, affordable. Can be colored through patination so an array of colored finishes are available.

Weaknesses When worn against the skin, will become discolored and oxidized, leaving a green residue. In jewelry making, use a combination of metals so that copper is not in contact with the skin.

Soldering When joining with silver, always consider where the join can be positioned discreetly as silver solder can stand out against the red of the copper. Sweat soldering or hidden seams will mask this. Copper solder is available but difficult to source. Copper solder will flow between two pieces of copper with no flux.

Buying Comes in various thicknesses and sizes of sheet, wire, and tubing. Purchase from specialist jewelry suppliers or hardware stores.

Brass
Brass is golden colored and as a metal is much harder and stronger than copper.

Usage It is often used to create fashion jewelry or coins and medals. Often rhodium or gold plated to offer an illusion of a higher valued metal.

Strengths Hard and strong. Combined with silver it is an affordable substitute for gold. Can be colored through patination allowing additional finish options.

Weaknesses When immersed in pickle solution, can develop a surface coating of copper, caused by residue from previously immersed pieces of silver. To avoid this, immerse brass in new, clean pickle solution and remove any copper residue with emery paper.

Soldering Same processes employed as for soldering silver. Brass solder paste available allowing discreet solder seams. Soldering achieved with a combination of flux and solder.

Buying Available in various sizes in sheet, wire, and tube form. Can be purchased from specialty metal suppliers or hardware stores.

Ferrous Metal
Stainless steel
The most commonly known ferrous metal applied in jewelry is stainless steel. Although not typically associated with jewelry this metal has become a popular material to use due to the low cost, the dark color, and the hardness of the metal.

Usage Particularly popular in men's jewelry, accessories, and watches. Commonly used for pins, fittings, and

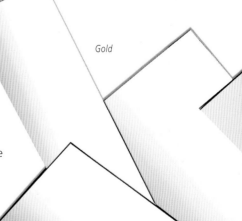

Gold

springs. Binding wire, jigs, clips, and tools are also often stainless steel.

Strengths Low cost, durable, hardwearing. Can be gold or rhodium plated to attain the appearance of higher value.

Weaknesses Hardness can make manipulation of the metal difficult. Annealing will make it easier to work with. Oxidization can occur rapidly preventing solder flow. Usual jewelry-making tools can become blunt quickly.

Soldering High temperatures and high-temperature-resistent flux should be used. Poor conductor of heat so heat source should be directed exactly on the solder join and work carried out quickly to avoid oxidization. Do not allow stainless steel to come into contact with pickle solution as the iron alloy will contaminate the solution.

Buying Comes in sheets, tubes, wire, and mesh. Purchasable from hardware stores and metal suppliers.

The brilliant white color of platinum and palladium make for beautiful and impressive jewelry.

Soldering Platinum and Palladium

Platinum and palladium are attractive metals because of their density and brilliant white color. A high heat is required when soldering them to allow the solder to flow.

Platinum and palladium are extremely strong and, combined with their reflective qualities, this makes them ideal for setting precious gemstones. Unlike white gold, they do not require rhodium plating. Although the cost of platinum is higher than that of 18 karat white gold, it requires no plating or replating, which is often required for white gold, and this balances out the initial higher cost.

When soldering platinum group metals (PGMs) such as palladium and platinum, ensure your torch is powerful enough to heat the metal and solder. Palladium and platinum have low thermal conductivity, which means heat should be focused directly at the soldering area, unlike metals such as silver.

Therefore, unlike gold and silver, with which there is danger of previously soldered joins flowing again when heated, platinum and palladium lend themselves well to multi-solder-join pieces.

Choose a background option that will reflect enough heat back: the most favorable surface is a high-temperature firebrick. An unclean workbench poses a danger of other metals, such as gold or silver particles, becoming embedded in the platinum or palladium. Always sweep and clean work and soldering stations when you have finished working with one metal. This also maintains separation of scrap and metal dusts for refining and recycling processes. And finally, when using any solders above medium grade, which therefore require the use of much higher temperatures which can be damaging to the eye, the use of welding glasses is an absolute necessity (with lenses from grade no. 5 to 10). These will prevent any damage to the eye, in particular to the retina.

Solder

For the range of solders available, see "Solders and Fluxes," pp 34–37. Palladium is the least dense and has the lowest melting point of the platinum group metals, between 2460°F and 2520°F (1350–1380°C), so hard and extra hard (1700) platinum solder should not be used. Platinum and palladium solder do not behave the same as silver: They are much more slow to flow. For this reason, joins must be accurately and tightly fitted to allow the flow of solder to successfully join the seam or parts together. It is best to apply many small paillons along a join with minimum spacing in between, reducing the risk of gaps. But in terms of quantity, surprisingly small amounts are sufficient.

Flux

As platinum does not oxidize when heated, it does not need a protective layer of flux, but using a flux will allow the solder to adhere to the seam area and reduce the risk of the solder flying off when flame is applied. Furthermore, a flux should be applied to lower-melting-point solders to protect them rather

Palladium and platinum are available in sheet, rod, wire, casting square, and solder panel form.

than the platinum. The recommended flux for this would be tenacity 5.

Exactly the same considerations apply to palladium. However, due to surface oxidization during heat-based repairs on finished pieces with gemstones or sensitive components, a ceramic flux can be applied to prevent discoloration; it is normally removable by heating with a gentle neutral flame or placing into pickle solution, neither of which is safe for finished gemstone-set pieces.

Heat-Proof Bricks

Highly heat-reflective bricks should be used. To keep these free from contamination, it is best to store them separately and use them exclusively for platinum or palladium soldering. However, if you prefer, charcoal bricks can offer sufficient heat and can be cleaned easily beforehand.

Heat Source

While using medium, easy, or extra easy to solder these metals, a general gas compressed air torch will provide sufficient heat. However, if you are working with hard or 1700 platinum solder, a higher heat source will be required. This is achievable from an oxy hydrogen torch (micro welder) or a conventional torch using oxy acetylene gas. A laser or PUK welder is also suitable if available, but this type of join is not as strong.

Soldering Palladium

During soldering of palladium using high-melting-temperature solders, the heat required oxidizes the metal surface into a black or bluish violet color. This color change does not affect the flow of solder and can be removed by heating the finished piece with a neutral flame or by immersing it in pickle solution. The heat from the soldering process can also make the palladium dull and remove its polished finish, but the normal procedures will return its shine.

Cleaning and Polishing

When cleaning, try to avoid using files to reduce the removal of these valuable metals and to avoid clogging up the files. For the same reason, always use the finest grade of abrasive or emery paper possible, going up to grade 1500 and applying the abrasive paper across the join. Abrasive and silicon wheels can also be applied to both platinum and palladium during the cleaning process.

If after cleaning platinum with emery paper, you find the solder seam is still quite visible, a tungsten burnisher can be used to disguise the area. This is made from an extremely hard metal and is able to work onto the platinum to visibly merge the filler and the platinum before polishing. To avoid visible solder seams altogether, it's possible to roll down a very thin piece of platinum section and insert it into a seam. It can be welded by micro welder, laser or PUK welder, or oxy acetylene torch. Once the piece has been joined, the excess metal can be filed and cleaned off to reveal an invisible seam. This technique allows a perfect color match and offers an invisible join, ideal for rings and bangles.

After cleaning properly, only a quick polish on the mops will be required. Always remember to cross polish, cutting across the solder join rather than following the direction of the seam. This will reduce the amount of solder that may be polished away, ultimately reducing the visibility of the solder seam. When a piece is constructed from platinum or palladium and a softer metal such as gold, it is best to polish the platinum before joining to the gold. The polishing compounds used for silver and gold can also be used for platinum group metals, but hyfin and white rouge work particularly well for them.

Solders and Fluxes

Solder is the metal filler that is used to join two parts together when soldering. To eliminate the build-up of oxide when heating metals, a coating of flux must be applied before soldering.

Tip

The color and exact melting point of solders may vary slightly from one supplier to another. To ensure your solder joins are uniform, it is best practice to use solder from only one source for any one jewelry piece.

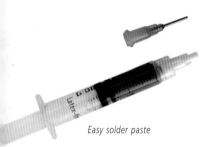

Easy solder paste

9kt extra easy gold solder

Solders

Solder has a lower melting point but similar properties to the metal it is joining. During the heating process of soldering, the structure of the parent metal changes and its internal crystals separate. This separation allows microscopic spaces to appear for the solder to flow into. This action makes solder joins particularly strong.

Before starting to use solder, there are many factors to consider. You will need to decide which hardness, color, and form of solder suits the task at hand. First of all, consider which hardness of solder you wish to use. This question can be answered by establishing the number of solder joins and evaluating the various melting temperatures of the solder types you will require. In addition, think about the color of the solder: The higher the melting point of solder, the closer it will match the metal in color. Finally, think about the solder form you wish to use, which will be determined by the soldering job. There is a varied selection to choose from—strip, wire, paste, or powder—each with its own unique properties (see pages 34 and 35).

A question often asked is how much solder to use. This is not an easy question to answer due to the fact that every solder join is individual and its solder requirements will vary. Often new jewelers make the mistake of applying excess solder. This miscalculation can cost valuable time in the removal and cleaning stage. It takes time and experience to learn the correct amount of solder to use and it can be a trial-and-error exercise until you become accustomed to soldering. As a general rule, it is better to use less and add extra if necessary than to use too much and spend long periods cleaning and removing. Before applying quantities of solder, ask yourself if the area can be cleaned easily. If not, take caution in the amount used. However, if a soldering area has easy access, then you can be more adventurous with the amount—but remember that the removal of excess solder will always be time-consuming.

Preparation

Always prepare solders and fluxes prior to the torch being switched on. Having snippets of solder at hand will ensure the soldering process is carried through smoothly. During soldering you will not have free hands with which to cut more paillons of solder.

The environment on which the solder is placed should be considered: Is it clean, has it been fluxed, and is it touching both surfaces for soldering? The size of the solder snippets should be smaller than the thickness of the metal you wish to solder. This allows the solder to melt easier and reduces the risk of the metal melting before the solder.

Melting Temperatures

Each grade of solder has a different melting temperature. Some metals have additional grades, but generally solders are available in hard, medium, easy, and extra easy. Hard melts at the highest temperature, and extra easy at the lowest temperature (see page 154).

As solder flows to the hottest area, you must ensure the solder area is heated evenly and that the flame is not pointed directly at the solder, as this would cause the solder to granulate into a ball. Furthermore, each time solder reaches melting temperature, a certain amount of the zinc contained will evaporate, causing the melting temperature of the solder to increase. This allows a jeweler to use the same hardness of solder for multiple joins without the risk of the piece collapsing. However, this increased melting temperature action can also have adverse effects: Overheating the solder can cause it to become brittle and porous, resulting in a weak, pitted solder seam. Therefore, it is important to withdraw heat as soon as the solder flows evenly.

Bear in mind that solder should be made from the same metal it is joining but alloyed with other, lower-melting-temperature metals to allow it to melt. Due to the fact that they are the same metal, the melting temperatures of the solder and the metal can be quite similar, so care has to be taken when heating an area for solder to avoid melting the metal.

The higher the melting point of solder, the greater the quantity of the matching metal, and thus the closer the color match. For example, easy and extra easy silver solders contain much less silver than hard solder and will produce a much more visible seam.

Silver solders are alloyed with copper and zinc. Solder strips come in different widths for each grade of solder and these vary depending on the specific supplier and country. This allows a jeweler to recognize the solder immediately.
• IT solder is an enamel solder and has the highest melting point. It will withstand the temperatures needed to heat enamel. Its melting point is very close to silver's, so precaution should be taken when using to avoid melting the piece.
• Hard solder is always used for the first solder joins as it has the highest melting temperature.
• Medium solder is used in the secondary stages of soldering when there are many solder joins to create.
• Easy solder should be applied only for the final solder join. It is mostly used for repairs where the soldering and solder-type history is unknown or close to an area where there is a risk of joins opening and collapsing.
• Extra easy should be applied only when completely necessary, where there is risk of damaging or affecting the stability of neighboring solder joins.

Gold solders are alloyed with metals such as copper, silver, zinc, tin, indium, and gallium. Additional alloys of silver, copper, and zinc are added to white gold solder. The grades are the same as for silver solder. Select a matching karat and color of gold. For gold-enameled pieces, very hard or hard solder (that does not contain zinc; enamel will not stick to zinc) should be applied to withstand the high kiln temperatures required to melt enamels.

Platinum solders are alloyed with various metals, such as palladium, gold, silver, copper, and zinc, depending on the grade. Although each supplier has their own formulae, names, and codes for platinum solder, the grades generally available are hard, medium, easy, and extra easy. In addition, a new solder called Platinum 1700 has recently been introduced. This has the closest color match and the lowest tendency to polish out, creating the least visible solder join. However, the melting temperature of this solder is very close to platinum's, so great care should be taken when soldering.

Palladium solders have recently appeared on the market, in hard, medium, and easy grades. However, palladium can be soldered with lower-melting-point platinum solders.

Solder Types

Solder strips are favored by jewelers due to the ease of cutting the desired thickness and size. If you have access, flattening the solder strip through a rolling mill can help with the cutting of paillons.

Solder wire can be used for stick feeding solder or for small areas and repairs. For higher-

Tip
As soon as solder has flowed successfully, remove the heat. Excess heat starts to burn out the zinc in the solder, and causes pinholes. Also, the more times solder is re-heated, the more likely it is to dry out or to start eating into the metal. If a piece requires further soldering in the same join or in a new seam, remove any excess solder with needle files or emery paper before applying new solder or re-heating for further joins.

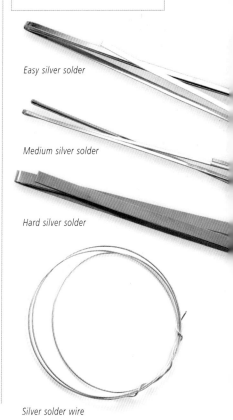

Easy silver solder

Medium silver solder

Hard silver solder

Silver solder wire

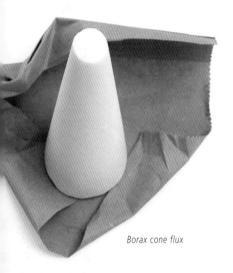

Borax cone flux

value solders, wire can be more affordable and available in smaller amounts. Wire can easily be cut into snippets.

Solder paste is a mixture of solder and flux that is dispensed from a syringe system. It is easy to use and time-saving, so, for repetitive soldering jobs such as chain soldering, it can have a great advantage. The accuracy of paste application reduces waste, so it is especially useful for high-karat gold solders. The disadvantages are weaker joins, paste's tendency to spread to unwanted areas, and the higher cost in comparison to other solder forms.

Solder panels are available for silver, gold, platinum, and palladium solders. These are thin sheets of solder that are easily cut with shears.

Solder powder is available in silver and gold. It is not commonly used but works well for intricate jewelry work such as filigree or granulation.

Fluxes

Flux must be applied to the entire solder area, as well as the solder itself. Flux enables the flow of solder by preventing oxides from forming on the surface of the metal. In addition, flux applied to the surface of silver or lower-karat golds can reduce the amount of fire-stain. A standard borax cone and dish will offer a flux that is sufficient for most soldering jobs, but it is beneficial to understand the various fluxes available and the types of metals and soldering jobs that they can assist with. As with solders, there are many types of fluxes to choose from and selecting the correct option will offer you the most favorable soldering surfaces and conditions for soldering.

Borax is available in powder or solid form. The powder form is simply mixed with water. When using the solid form, the cone is ground against a coarse dish of water in a circular movement, until it forms a paste. The paste is painted onto solder joins and seams with a clean brush. This commonly used flux is cost-effective and offers the jeweler control in the consistency of the

How To Cut Solder Paillons

Before you start soldering, during the set-up process it is a good idea to pre-cut some solder snippets into the flux dish in preparation. This will allow easy and quick access. Also cut additional pieces as you may need extra just at the vital soldering stage. It is important to ensure solder is clean and uncontaminated before use, so clean if necessary. It is not advisable to place soldering into pickle solution.

BEWARE: If you are using multiple grades of solder, do not cut and mix them together in the dish. Once cut it is difficult to distinguish the grade of solder.

1 Using sharp straight shears, cut along the length of the solder strip. It depends on the width of the piece, but on a standard hard silver solder strip, four equally wide sections can be cut.

2 Once the four sections have been cut along the length they become curved. Flatten them again with your hands, pushing the strip flat against the top of the work bench or use flat nose pliers to flatten.

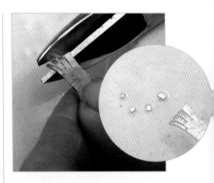

3 With the shears, cut across the four strips over the flux dish. Not only will this be a safe place to keep the solder pieces, but they will also be coated in flux which is required for soldering.

flux. In addition, the dish is an ideal container for housing cut solder paillons.

Enamel fluxes are available specifically for this type of jewelry technique.

Liquid flux is useful for gold and silver soldering but is predominately used for gold. This flux does not expand when heated, reducing the risk of solder and parts disjoining. There is no need to prepare it, and it is easy to use and apply. It is ideal for intricate soldering work, be it gold or small links.

Easy Flo works best for low-melting-temperature solders, so it is ideal for easy or extra easy solder.

Tenacity 5 is best applied for mid to high temperatures. To use, mix it into a paste with water and paint it onto the solder area. When heated, this type of flux becomes difficult to remove—it can only be done with abrasive tools such as emery papers.

Application of flux is important too. Just as all areas and components for soldering must be clean, so must the flux. Make sure the borax dish or container of any liquid flux is clean, as well as the brush. There is no point spending time fitting and cleaning the components for solder only to use an unclean brush, dish, or container which will inevitably contaminate the flux, solder area, and solder,

preventing successful flow of solder. When heat is applied to borax ground flux, the water contained will start to bubble and evaporate; then the flux swells and starts to turn white. Carefully continue to apply heat with the bushy part of the flame to avoid displacing the pieces of solder. Finally, the flux should turn shiny and glassy, coating and protecting the metal. At this point the solder will begin to flow. If the solder does not flow, the heat from the torch will start to burn away the flux, so another coat must be applied. All fluxes must be used in a well-ventilated area.

How To Prepare Borax Cone Flux

Before you start, you will need a coarse dish, some clean water, and a clean brush.

Tip

After time the borax paste will dry out. To revitalize, wet the paste with a wet brush or pour in a small amount of water and grind again. The more use the borax dish gets, the easier it will become to produce more paste.

1 Pour clean water into the dish, only a small amount first. Excess water will make it more difficult to grind and, as the dish is very shallow you will find excess water spills out.

2 Take the borax cone and start grinding in a circular motion as well as side to side. Apply heavy pressure downward on the cone.

3 Continue grinding until the water has a paste-like consistency. A clean brush can be used to paint this onto the solder piece.

Setting Up Your Workstation

The area where soldering is carried out must be set up correctly. Bear in mind not only the safety of the soldering station, but also the positioning of your equipment.

Prepare Your Tools and Yourself

Position all the tools required for your task at a comfortable height and close at hand for speedy and easy reach. As well as the tools immediately required, bear in mind other essentials too. For example, is there cool water close by or within easy reach to quench hot metals; are the flux dishes and solder paillons ready; can you reach a range of tweezers? Remember that if you are in the middle of a crucial solder join you will not want to move from the soldering station to grab a tool you have placed far out of reach. Whether sitting or standing, comfort is a must for a jeweler. If you are uncomfortable, then it is likely the soldering will be unsuccessful. As soldering requires precise and accurate work, the jeweler must be in a position that facilitates steady hands and accurate movements.

A workstation set up for soldering with the torch positioned and securely held by a hook at the side of the bench. The soldering area is protected at the back with the upright firebrick, which additionally reflects heat back on to the soldering area. An overhead light has been positioned above the bench peg area and can be accessed and switched off easily during the soldering process.

Think About Your Lighting

During the preparation of pieces prior to soldering, the ideal lighting is white and clear. You need to see the pieces clearly in order to achieve the cleanest and tightest of fits. However, when soldering begins, all overhead lights should be switched off to allow the jeweler to view the metal color change during the process. The changing color of metals provides a good indication of temperature, allowing you to know when the optimum temperature for solder flow has been achieved.

It is also advisable to use the same lighting conditions on each occasion you solder to avoid confusion in identifying the differing metal color changes. However, ensure the dimmed lighting you choose is sufficient to work safely. Of course, once soldering has been successfully carried out, turn the lighting back on. Lighting preference may change as you become more confident with metal color change and other indicators of solder flow.

Practice Using Your Tools

The torch is the key piece of equipment required for soldering (see pages 22–25). To get optimum use from a torch, learn about the workings of it and become comfortable and confident by practicing holding it, turning it on and off, and testing the flame on scrap metals. Beginner jewelers often find the torch a frightening tool to use: The release of the flame can seem overpowering and daunting initially, but practicing on scrap metals will allow you to become more confident and at ease. As with any piece of jewelry equipment, the jeweler must feel in control of it.

Also take time to get comfortable holding both the torch and tweezers. Tweezers should be held with the hand you write with, as this will give you the best control, and the torch held with the opposite hand.

As solder flows to the hottest area, it is crucial to understand the workings of the torch and the flame. Learning which part of the flame produces the most heat, how to adjust the flame, and when to apply and withdraw heat, is imperative to the use of the torch. These skills can only be achieved with time and practice.

The majority of jewelers tend to become accustomed and comfortable with the use of one particular type of torch. Although most soldering jobs are achievable with standard gas torches, there are occasions when a different variety will be required. This may be when a high-melting-point solder is required or very detailed fine work is being carried out. Therefore, it is best to determine the type of heat, flame, and torch required before you start any soldering, although standard jewelry torches can be fitted with various sizes of heads to adapt the flow of the flame.

Always bear in mind that blow torches are safe as long as they have been set up by an expert and are used correctly, with safety procedures in mind. Refer to an expert and the torch manual for safety protocols prior to use.

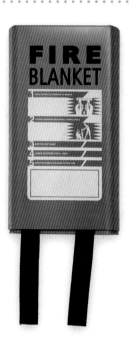

Fire-safety equipment should be maintained and easily accessible. Fire blankets are a must when open flames are in use, as is a heat-resistant bowl containing cool water to allow immersion and cooling of hot pieces.

Planning Your Construction

During the design stage of your pieces, give thought to their construction. This is the time to work out a list of parts and consider your soldering stages.

¹⁄₂ in (11mm)

¹⁄₂₅ in (1mm) thick

¹⁄₃ in (15mm)

Toggle wire the same as the cloud

Final solder points

Plans to make the cloud from one piece of wire were later abandoned during construction in favor of individually fabricated and soldered pieces.

Hand make tapered bezel setting

Cloud part: score, fold, and solder. Square wire.

Approx ¹⁄₃ in (9mm)

1¹⁄₈ in (29mm)

2¹⁄₄ in (53mm)

3 drops, individually solder before applying to cloud part. May apply medium solder if necessary.

Raindrops ¹⁄₈ × ¹⁄₄ in (3.5 × 6mm)

During the early stages of the design process, develop a list of parts you will need. This should include dimension guidelines for the piece and will enable you to plan out the metals and materials required. Include in your plan a construction and component list, which when numbered can form a guide or map of the piece, allowing you to know the exact soldering stages and steps required. This will offer an easy-to-follow guide, allowing the jeweler to plan the types of solders to apply and when.

When constructing a piece, always work first with the largest components, as they require more heat, and then work your way down in terms of size and location of pieces. For example, if you are constructing a large piece made from several parts and then a variety of smaller components, it makes sense to solder all the large parts and then to work on the smaller pieces. This means the jeweler can start with the hardest solder, which takes the most intense heat, and by the time they are soldering the smaller items they have worked down to medium or easy solder, which requires less heat to melt and in turn avoids problems with melting of smaller parts.

Of course, as with any type of construction, steps can change during the production process, but knowing in advance the steps required makes work easier for the jeweler. Remember that good planning means that you will use the appropriate hardness of solder at the right time. If medium or easy solder is applied when there are many more solder joins to complete, it can cause problems with joins opening and the construction collapsing.

Solder Seams

During design, think about where solder can be avoided—are there parts that can be constructed from one piece rather than two soldered pieces? If it is possible to make a part from one piece rather than soldering many, avoid solder whenever you can.

Also think about the strength of the solder join. Ultimately you want to achieve the strongest join and avoid weakness. To do so, thought should be given to the amount of solder surface area and the fit of the two pieces: A stronger connection could be created if the pieces were slotted together prior to soldering. Finally, consider where you can hide solder joins. If there are many components and parts to one piece, it may be best to apply a solder join where it can be hidden or less noticeable.

From sketch to finished piece
One of Wing Mun Devenney's working drawings (left) for her cloud pendant, shown above. The soldering of the three raindrops onto the cloud part was difficult due to the fine chain against the heavier weight wire of the cloud. Due to the difference in metal thickness, during soldering there was a risk of the chain melting before the solder flowed. However, Wing Mun managed to solder successfully without having to use a lower-melting-temperature solder.

Preparing Parts and Joins

Solder will flow into a heated channel by capillary action. In order to achieve this successfully, the join or seam you wish to solder must be a close, tight fit.

To prepare and produce an ideal fit between pieces, piercing and filing will be required. Filing is perhaps one of the most monotonous jewelry-making tasks, but despite its tediousness it is essential prior to soldering. Established piercing and filing techniques will allow the jeweler to create a solid channel for solder to flow and to fit metals and joins together well. The most effective method to ensure the seam for soldering is a tight fit is to check against light: If light is sweeping through, there is too much of a gap.

If the parts for soldering are to be applied on top of one another, such as flat sheet to flat sheet, the two pieces should be as flush together as possible, with all surface areas touching each other to allow the solder to join them. If soldering round wires parallel to one another, ensure they sit tightly flush to one another with no gaps. Always bear in mind whatever two surfaces you are soldering, be they round, flat, or shaped, that the two pieces should always fit tightly together and have as large a solder surface as possible. To achieve this may require a substantial amount of cutting and filing, but inevitably this preparation will save you time and allow the solder to flow successfully.

Solder should not be used to fill gaps and a jeweler must never try to flood a join, as this could result in the solder eating into the metal instead. This will cause irreversible consequences and can be difficult or impossible to repair. Furthermore, a solder join that has been created with excess flooding of solder will be a weak join that can break easily. Bear in mind that preparation time of solder seams and joins should by far outweigh soldering duration. Thought needs to be given to the soldering of tubing or metal parts that are prone to metal relaxation or size change during the heating process: Annealing should be carried out to avoid excess metal movement. This is the process of heating metal to soften it so that it can be worked on, hammered, or formed more easily. This would also apply to a piece that has been worked on prior to soldering and that has become work-hardened.

Cleaning of Parts

When parts have been filed and fitted perfectly together, the next stage is to remove any dirt, oil residue, carbon, or oxides that may have formed from previous heating of the metal. Solder flows into clean spaces, and any areas that are not cleaned properly may hinder or reduce the flow of the solder. When using new metal, the parts should be relatively clean and blemish-free but parts that have been worked on will require cleaning. Metal may also require cleaning with emery paper or a similar tool, if the areas for soldering are large—sanding will create a cleaner and more suitable surface for solder to flow.

An effective method of cleaning metal is in a pickle solution. Once removed from the solution, rinse with water to remove any residue, then ensure minimum contact with your hands to avoid contamination with grease—the best option for holding a piece is tweezers. A sure method of checking for grease marks is to place the piece under running water. If the water runs off smoothly, it is grease free, but if its flows in droplets then there is a residue of grease that still has to be removed prior to soldering.

Metal can also be cleaned with emery paper, wire brushes, files, or a scraper, all of which remove the top surface of the metal to reveal a cleaner surface below, ready for soldering work.

As with the parts, the solder should also be cleaned if necessary, using the same tools as described to ensure it is uncontaminated—new pieces of solder generally do not require this. However, it is not advisable to place solder in pickle solution.

Be Prepared

- If your piece has multiple solder joins, do not clean and finish the piece (or any joins) until the final join has been completed. This allows previously soldered joins to flow when reheated and accommodates any possible movement of parts. If you pierce, file, and clean an already soldered seam, the parts cannot move and solder cannot flow. Time spent cleaning components may well be wasted at this stage as parts may become fire-stained or marked as soldering continues.
- Always bear in mind that if you intend to solder a frame onto a base sheet, the back plate should be slightly larger. This allows for movement and for solder to flow around the outer edge. Once successfully soldered, the additional metal can be pierced away and the outer edge cleaned of any excess solder.

Holding Small Parts

When positioning pieces on your soldering area, make sure that you set them up securely so they are stable and unlikely to move.

If your components move during soldering, they can be soldered in the wrong position or collapse. To repair and remove incorrectly soldered parts is both damaging to the piece and extremely time-consuming, so, if you feel there is room for movement, take the time to find a position that is steady and secure.

Bear in mind the law of gravity and base your set-up around this. For example, if you are preparing to solder a rub-over setting onto a ring shank, instead of balancing the setting on the top of the ring, it is more stable to turn the setting upside down and to place the ring shank on top, held in place with reverse-action tweezers. Consider what equipment—be it tweezers, binding wire, or pins—can assist in the positioning of the pieces and offer the most stable support. Of course, whatever you decide to use, keep in mind that the equipment can become a heat sink and draw away heat from an area that you do not wish it to be near, so try to hold a piece where withdrawing heat will not affect the join you are soldering.

Positioning Yourself

Almost as important as the position of the piece is the position of the jeweler. Place yourself in an area where you feel the most comfortable and are able to view the soldering area easily and at the best angle. Ensure whatever position you are in allows you to have both hands steady and free to offer the precise work that soldering needs.

Using Binding Wire

Binding wire is available in various sizes, so choose according to the size of your parts and pieces. Take time and care when using binding wire that the parts have been secured in the correct position and bound well enough to offer good support during soldering. If binding wire becomes soldered to your piece, unwind it and grab close to the soldered end with pliers—then pull once with force. This will detach the wire from the piece and, if any marks have been left, they can be removed by light filing.

Kinks can be made in the wire by twisting it around round nosed pliers. This allows for expansion of the metal and prevents any marks from the wire.

Binding wire can be used to secure lengths of wire for soldering. The wire prevents the pieces from falling away from each other when the metal expands during heating.

During the soldering of a tube or bezel, the heat will cause the metal to expand and on occasion the join will open. To prevent this, bind and secure tubing along its length, not forgetting to add kinks on the wire.

Soldering long pieces together can prove challenging, especially when trying to keep the two pieces securely united along the entire length. Binding wire can be used to join the two.

A stone setting or component can be held and secured onto the main body of a piece before placing onto the soldering station. This bezel setting has been bound to the shank with fine binding wire.

Using Reverse-Action Tweezers

Wooden-handled reverse-action tweezers are extremely useful for holding pieces close to the solder area during soldering.

As the solder runs, release the tweezers and the piece will stick to the running solder.

Earring posts can be positioned and held in place with a balanced pair of reverse-action tweezers.

Reverse-action tweezers can be used to hold and secure any type of finding or fitting, such as holding cufflink backs onto a curved surface.

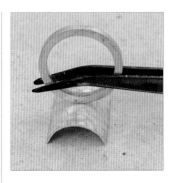

To position a curved shank against a curved surface, first file the two surfaces to create a closer and stronger join. The shank can then be held in place with a pair of reverse-action tweezers.

When soldering on a curved surface, it is best to prop the main body of the piece against broken fragments of firebrick, so you can solder on a flat plane. If you are unable to do this, then hold the piece, such as a brooch fitting, with a pair of reverse-action tweezers.

Reverse-action tweezers come in handy for holding in place a jump ring within a chain. A position that frees the join from touching any part of another jump ring can be created.

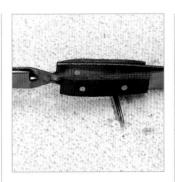

Reverse-action tweezers can often become unbalanced. To ensure they are sitting securely, pins can be placed underneath.

Tip

When you are holding with reverse-action tweezers, take care to avoid melting and pushing findings and fittings together, which could ruin the mechanism.

Using Wire Supports

Wire supports offer stability and security for parts which may otherwise move or become parted during the soldering process.

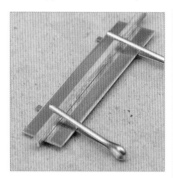

Clips and pins are useful to hold lengthy pieces together during soldering. These cotter split pins have been applied to secure the heavy square wire flat against the base sheet in preparation for soldering.

Supports can be adapted into a pedestal or base on which a non-flat piece can sit. The round, curved top of this cotter pin is ideal for positioning a domed piece.

A cotter pin has been cut and the ends pulled apart slightly to allow the domed part of a cufflink to remain stationed at an angle.

A large cotter pin has been shortened and pulled apart slightly to create a platform on which the sheet metal is raised to the right level for soldering to the round bezel.

Using Pins

Pins are placed into the soldering surface, be it firebrick or charcoal block, to secure parts in position or keep them upright.

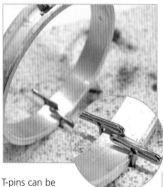

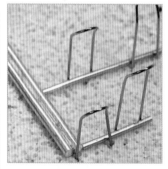

T-pins can be pushed through firebricks to create a holder that can position a piece—such as a bangle—upright. T-pins can also be pushed into a brick and bent over to grip a piece down, which is especially useful if you have made a mistake and are trying to un-solder one piece from another.

Jewelry display pins can be used to hold pieces upright, as when you wish to solder a piece onto the top section of a ring shank.

When soldering fine wire pieces, the air from the torch can cause movement. To avoid this, pins can be pushed through the brick to hold the pieces securely.

When positioning an item with a curved base on a brick surface, movement is a risk. Try putting a pin into the brick, then placing a curved piece, like this domed cufflink, over the top.

Using Soldering Surfaces

There are many types of soldering surfaces to work on. It is vital to understand how each surface can be used, as well as how to combine it with jigs such as pins or binding wire.

Prior to any soldering work, think about the metal and the type of work you are trying to achieve before planning the surface to use. Consider the temperatures that will be applied and the type of set-up that is required. Although the commonly used magnesia soldering brick can be sufficient for most types of soldering, you may find further benefits in other options.

There are a variety of heat-proof bricks and surfaces, each offering their own benefits to a soldering job (see page 26 and pages 46–47). Consider which would be most suitable for the type of soldering you wish to achieve before you set up the pieces.

Elevating Pieces

As fire-proof soldering surfaces can absorb some of the heat from a torch, when soldering a large or heavy metal piece, having the piece raised will allow optimum heat distribution. Allowing air to circulate freely will also help with the soldering. When soldering an area where larger and smaller components meet, by raising the larger pieces you are able to heat your surface evenly and to an optimum temperature before applying heat to the smaller components, thus avoiding overheating the smaller sections. Elevate parts whenever necessary by supporting them on pieces of heat-proof brick or on other supporting props such as a wire rack or soldering wig.

Using a Revolving Turntable

During soldering, it is often necessary to gain access to all sides and angles of the piece to deliver even heat distribution. For this purpose, the spinning action of the turntable is perfect. This is a strong, heavy base housing a turntable. A heatproof surface (such as a firebrick) is placed on top of the turntable prior to soldering parts being placed. This acts to protect the turntable from heat and also provides an optimum soldering surface.

As this bezel setting is soldered, the turntable is rotated to allow the jeweler 360-degree visibility. As the solder flows, the piece is rotated (see how the seam is moved on in a clockwise direction) so the solder can flow evenly around the whole piece.

Using Soldering Sheets

Soldering sheets are a good size for protecting the soldering station from excess heat. The disadvantage of using these sheets is that they are more likely to become damaged and start to disintegrate much faster than other options.

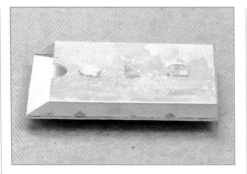

Tip

This large sheet can also be positioned behind the soldering station to protect the background area.

This soldering surface can be placed onto a turntable or workbench, and soldering can be carried out directly from the surface.

Pieces can be broken or sawed off to prop and lift piece off the surface to allow heat to circulate beneath the piece.

Using Magnesia Soldering Block

This is possibly the most commonly used soldering base due to its lightweight and soft qualities. Due to the softness of this brick, it can be easily cut and carved into.

Using the end of a pair of tweezers or other flat, blunt-ended metal tools, a hole can be carved.

Curved based pieces can be placed into a hole, allowing the piece to sit securely with low risk of movement during soldering.

Pins can be applied with ease to prop and secure parts in place.

Again, sawed-off or broken pieces can be used to prop parts up or hold them in place.

Using Charcoal Bricks

Charcoal bricks are strong heat reflectors and can be adapted for many uses. They are particularly suited to use with metals with high melting temperatures, such as platinum and palladium.

Prior to the first use, bind the sides of the charcoal brick with several coils of binding wire. This will secure it and prevent it from breaking apart when heated.

Charcoal is quite a workable material and pins can be easily inserted to hold parts and pieces in place for soldering. Here, stainless jewelry display pins have been inserted to hold the ring in a steady upright position.

Pieces of charcoal can be sawed or broken off and placed below parts to lift the pieces off the surface. This will allow heat to access the base of the piece.

Tip
Always have a water spray bottle at hand to spritz the brick and prevent further burning after the heating or soldering process.

Using Asbestos Substitute Soldering Bricks

Due to their smooth, flat surface, these heat-proof blocks are particularly useful for soldering pieces that require a flat base.

Placing a brick behind a flat brick will allow heat to reflect back onto the piece. This creates a good heat reflector and additionally protects the background area.

Place two bricks side-by-side and use the gap between the two as a channel with which to position parts for soldering. Additionally, two bricks can be employed in this way to hold pieces in an upright position.

Using Honeycomb Board

The high heat resistance of this soldering surface makes it durable and long-lasting. The surface of the board is completely covered with holes that reflect heat back onto the piece being soldered.

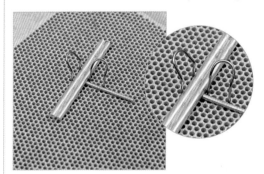

With holes across the entire surface, pins can be easily inserted to hold pieces in place.

Solder Inhibitors and Heat Insulators

Regardless of experience, even the most highly skilled jeweler will on occasion use solder inhibitors and heat insulators. Both are useful to have on hand in any jeweler's workshop.

Through time and practice, most jewelers can master the technique of soldering a multi-joined piece without an unwanted solder join opening or moving. Jewelers may apply heat away from an area; use heat sinks to draw heat away; not apply flux to an area to create oxidization, thus preventing solder from flowing; or use a lower-melting-temperature solder. However, these techniques may still pose a risk to the piece—and on these occasions solder inhibitors become a useful tool.

Gemstones and non-metal materials are generally applied to a jewelry piece in the final stage of manufacture, thus preventing heat damage. However, during the repair of a piece, the non-metal components may be too fragile to unset or remove, and soldering work may have to be carried out with the parts still attached. It is then that a heat-insulating coating can be added to a component or material for protection.

Although the methods described here are tried and tested, there is no 100 percent guarantee the area or component is protected and safe. As with other areas of jewelry making, even the most experienced jeweler can accidentally damage a piece.

Beware that some solder inhibitors can contaminate the pickle solution, so any applied should be washed off with warm soap solution and a soft brush before immersing in the pickle solution.

There are a number of solder inhibitors and heat insulators:

Heat insulating gel can be applied over a stone. Once the soldering has been completed, leave the piece to cool before placing in water. Clean the coating off prior to placing in pickle solution.

Rouge is commonly used as a polishing compound and is available in both powder and cake form. It can also be a very effective and low-cost solder inhibitor. The cake can be heated and, when in paste form, applied liberally to a stone. Rouge powder can be mixed with water and applied to a particular area to prevent solder from running.

Powered chalk can be ground and mixed with a small amount of water.

Yellow ochre powder is mixed with water or alcohol.

Pencil lead can be drawn around the area you do not wish the solder to flow.

Here we look at the uses and application of rouge as a solder inhibitor. Always work in a well-ventilated room.

Using Rouge Mix

Tip
It is possible to use borax to protect a diamond from heat during soldering. Apply borax over the diamond's surface, ensuring the coating is thick. Once soldering is complete, allow the piece to cool, as quenching will cause damage.

1 Place some rouge powder into a small clean dish. Pour in a small amount of clean water.

2 Using a clean brush, mix the water and the powder together, slowly adding more water if necessary. Continue to blend until a creamy mixture has been achieved.

3 Paint the mixture carefully onto pre-soldered joins that you wish to prevent from flowing. Take care not to contaminate any other areas where you wish solder to flow.

Applications of Rouge Solder Inhibitor

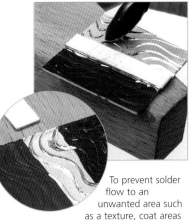

To prevent solder flow to an unwanted area such as a texture, coat areas by painting on solder inhibitor. Solder will not flow into the rouge-covered areas, thus preventing the texture from being flooded with molten solder. Once the coating of solder inhibitor has dried, the remaining areas or pieces for soldering can be painted with flux.

To prevent solder running into catches or clasps which require free movement, use a solder inhibitor. Paint the top area of a brooch fitting, leaving the base area to be coated with flux and allowing solder to flow.

Protect stones or other non-metal parts from heat damage by applying heat-resistant gel or rouge. This applies to soldering repairs when removing the stones could cause damage. When heat-resistant coatings are applied to a part or stone, allow the piece to cool thoroughly after soldering. Any sudden temperature changes can impact on the stone and cause the piece to shatter.

Warning: Please note that there are no guarantees in preventing damage to parts or stones. Heat-resistant gels and pastes will reduce the risk dramatically but, as with any form of jewelry making, on occasion damage can occur. If possible, reduce the risk by not applying direct heat to any heat-sensitive materials.

Note

When using any type of solder inhibitor, be vigilant about cleaning areas after use. Any remaining traces could contaminate other parts or areas where you wish solder to flow.

4 Leave a space between the base and the dome so optimum soldering temperature can be reached around the seam and surrounding areas. Allow the rouge paste to dry.

5 Prepare and flux the joins you wish to solder as normal, placing paillons of solder where required. Heat the area for soldering as normal and allow solder to flow before removing heat.

6 Once the piece has cooled, clean with soapy water and a soft brush prior to placing in pickle solution. Never place rouge-coated pieces in pickle solution as this will cause contamination.

Chapter 2
Key Soldering Techniques

This chapter offers step-by-step directions for mastering a range of standard soldering techniques. We begin with simple techniques, such as butt soldering, and progress to more complex procedures, such as stick feed soldering. This selection of techniques will give the jeweler a platform of skills that will allow the fabrication and successful soldering of silver, gold, platinum, and palladium pieces.

Once followed and learned, you can adapt the techniques for your own designs or for manufacturing the projects offered later in this book. All the expert tips offered will assist you as you begin to work on a range of soldering tasks.

ESSENTIAL TOOLS
For every technique you will need:

- Shears for cutting solder paillons
- Borax dish to hold snippets of solder
- Stainless steel tweezers for placing solder paillons
- A revolving turntable, though not essential, is always useful for accessing all angles of your piece
- A firebrick or other suitable surface for soldering on
- Torch
- A dish of cool water for quenching
- Pickle solution
- A selection of needle files and various grades of emery paper. Specific grades or files may be mentioned in individual tools lists

Sweat Soldering

Sweat soldering joins two surfaces, one on top of the other. It is practiced often and is ideal for seams where solder is difficult to apply and also for flat to flat surfaces, such as sheet metal.

TOOLS AND MATERIALS
* Silver sheet
* Rawhide mallet
* Flat stake
* Selection of fine and coarse emery papers
* Borax cone, dish, and brush
* Hard silver solder

SKILL LEVEL 💍

This is an easy soldering technique in which the top piece has solder sweated onto its surface area, before being placed upside down on the lower piece. It offers a clean join that does not require the positioning of solder paillons along the seams of two pieces. As the top piece has solder pre-applied and melted, the positioning of the top piece can be carried out easily and accurately.

The most important preparation for sweat soldering is to ensure that the two surfaces for soldering will be flat against each other. For flat sheets you may need to anneal and tap both surfaces gently with a mallet against a flat stake.

If the pieces are not of sheet form, such as wire or carved metal, it would be best to achieve a slightly flat surface by rubbing against coarse emery paper.

When applying the solder to the top piece, place the paillons close to the edge. Not only will this create a smooth, clean join but also allow the jeweler to see the solder running and determine at which point to remove the heat. When embarking on the solder of the two pieces, always apply heat to the larger piece first and then gently bring the flame onto both, creating an even temperature that will allow the solder to flow between.

FLEUR AQUA BRACELET
JO MARKWICK
Use of sweat soldering techniques allows the intricate detailing on this top-level pattern to be soldered securely. By sweat soldering onto the base surface, the jeweler ensures that the fine details are not flooded with excess solder.

Sweat Soldering Guidelines

• For a tight and precise fit, make sure the two pieces are as flat as possible, allowing the surfaces to meet flush for solder to flow. To flatten, tap with a mallet against a flat stake or surface.

• Ensure the two surfaces are clean and oil-free to allow the solder to flow.

1 Cut both pieces for soldering. Check they are flat and flush against each other. If they are not completely flush, anneal both (see page 41) and gently tap with a mallet against a flat stake.

2 With fine emery paper, sand the top of the large piece and the base of the small piece. This will offer a more stable and clean surface for solder to flow. Clean off any dust particles under running water.

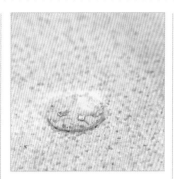

3 Apply a coat of borax cone flux to the base of the smaller piece, before using tweezers to place small paillons of hard solder close to the edges. Heat on a firebrick with a small, gentle neutral flame, circling the entire area until the solder runs. Allow to cool before quenching and placing in pickle solution.

4 Once the piece is cleaned and dried, use coarse emery paper to sand the surface of the solder to remove any solder lumps and to give a flatter surface. This will allow the piece to sit flush and flat on top of the larger base sheet.

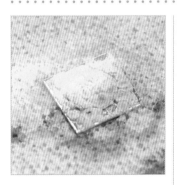

5 Flux both pieces well and place the round piece in position, upside down on top of the larger piece, with the solder in between the two parts. Place the pieces on a firebrick on a turntable and, with the flame, heat both pieces gently to dry the flux and allow the expansion to stop.

6 Using the flame, direct heat to the base sheet first, and then move it toward the disc. Circle the flame around both and, as the two pieces start to turn dull red, the solder will flow. Direct the solder by concentrating the flame along the join. Revolve the turntable to see all angles and to check the solder has flowed completely round the disc.

7 Wait for at least a minute, until the metal is no longer glowing, then quench and place the piece in pickle solution. Sweat soldering produces minimal excess solder, so very little cleaning should be required. The solder seam should be clean and neat.

The two pieces are joined perfectly together with a clean and tidy solder seam. Furthermore, this type of solder join produces minimal excess solder.

TOOLS AND MATERIALS

* Two pieces of silver sheet
* Large flat file
* Rawhide mallet
* Flat stake
* Scribe
* Engineer's set square
* Borax cone, dish, and brush
* Hard silver solder

SKILL LEVEL ♦

Butt Soldering

Butt soldering is when two pieces are soldered edge to edge or at a right angle to each other. This common technique is used between flat to flat, flat to curve, or curve to curve surfaces.

There are countless examples of where butt joins are used, including: the join in a jump ring, the ends of a closed bangle, a bale to a pendant, or a piece of tube onto a flat sheet. Due to the fact that this type of solder join can have less surface area of solder and attachment, creating a weak point in the construction of the piece, it is wise to think about how to strengthen the join before you solder, whether by increasing the solder surface area or by removing metal so the two pieces can be slotted into one another.

In the example of a jump ring, a slight groove should be filed for the ring to fit into. This not only increases the surface area for solder but also makes the fit more flush, allowing the solder to flow more successfully. This results in a much stronger solder join. Another method of strengthening the join is to carve or remove a section where the butt ends meet. For example, earring post solder joins can be drilled and the post inserted to give a stronger connection, as well as holding the post in place during soldering.

LINKED LEAF BRACELET

ROBERT FEATHER

Each leaf shape in this piece has been formed from square wire and then butt soldered together. By filing the piece, the designer has created a large soldering surface area and clean sharp lines in the leaf shapes. The additional silver and gold leaves and the jump rings linking the components together were also butt soldered. The matte finish to this necklace really highlights the color difference between the silver and the yellow gold.

1 Cut and form one of the pieces of rectangular silver sheet into a ring shank. This will need to stand flush on the other piece of silver sheet. Check by eye that the two edges of the ring shank are flat: If not, work with a large flat file.

2 Check if light creeps through the join, which will allow you to determine if it is a tight fit. If light does pass through, the gap is too large for solder to flow successfully. The closer and better the fit, the higher the chance of successful soldering.

3 If you find the flat sheet has an irregular surface and does not quite fit flat against the ring shank, then anneal and tap with a mallet against a flat metal stake.

4 Once the two pieces have been fitted and matched up, use a scribe and engineer's square to measure and mark a line on either side of the flat piece. These marks will indicate where the ring shank should be positioned and aligned for soldering.

5 Paint borax flux onto the top surface of the flat sheet and the edges of the shank. To prevent excess build-up of fire-stain, flux can be applied to the complete surfaces of both pieces if desired.

6 Position the flat piece on a firebrick, then turn the ring shank upside down and align it with the scribe marks. Apply fluxed paillons of hard solder onto the insides of both edges, which will keep the visible outer seam as clean and neat as possible.

7 Using a medium-sized neutral flame, heat the base and the shank area. Once the flux has dried, direct the flame to the base sheet, before concentrating on the shank area. Move the flame in a semi-circular action around the shank to allow even heat distribution.

8 Use a turntable to direct the flame to all sides. As the pieces start to change to dull red, focus the flame on one seam. Allow the flame to heat evenly along the inside and outer edge of the join as you want the solder to flow completely along the seam.

9 Once the solder runs, you should be able to view a clean bright line. Now direct the flame onto the second solder join. Repeat the process, drawing the flame along the seam internally and externally until the solder flows right along it.

10 When solder runs smoothly and evenly along the second seam, remove the heat. Allow the piece to cool for at least a minute before quenching in water and immersing in pickle solution.

Applying solder onto the inside of both seams has produced clean and neat visible outer joins. The excess solder on the inside can be cleaned with fine needle files or emery paper.

Soldering Jump Rings

Both jump rings and pre-made chains are readily available to purchase, but knowing how to make and solder jump rings allows the jeweler to produce them quickly, adapt to any length or style, and match their designed piece.

TOOLS AND MATERIALS

* Pre-made or purchased silver jump rings
* Stainless steel ruler
* Two pairs of flat nosed pliers, straight or angled
* Liquid flux and clean brush
* Borax cone and dish (see right)
* Hard silver solder strip
* Straight-ended stainless steel tweezers
* Reverse-action tweezers
* Emery paper
* Tumble polisher or polishing mops

SKILL LEVEL 💍 💍

Jump Ring Guidelines

• Preparation of the jump rings is vital to the success of the solder. Jump rings should be cut only with saw blades and not snipes or shears, as these will not create a flat plane for joins.

• Wire solder is useful for tipping the solder join of a jump ring, which can speed up soldering. Whether you are using strip or wire, positioning snippets of solder onto small jump rings takes practice.

• Paste solder with flux is normally available in syringe form. This option allows accurate placement of the solder with the flux already mixed in, thus saving time. In a commercial environment, paste solder is often used for chain repairs.

Jump rings are simple to construct: Using very few tools and a variety of wire sizes and shapes, a jeweler can create a wide range, offering an array of links for chain-making too. Although chain-making is quite time-consuming and standard chains can be purchased easily, possessing the skills to manufacture chains eliminates the problem of sourcing a completely matching style of chain for your pieces.

The actual soldering of jump rings can prove to be a challenge. Learning to apply the right amount of heat, not melting the piece, and mastering soldering without running into areas you do not wish, will endow a jeweler with an array of fundamental skills they can utilize in other soldering techniques.

You can use only liquid flux for this technique. However, as the dish is ideal for housing solder paillons, here I have applied liquid flux to the pieces and fluxed the solder with ground borax.

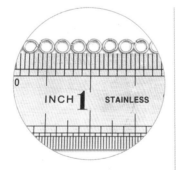

1 Taking some pre-made or purchased jump rings, determine the length of chain and the number of jump rings you need by aligning and measuring against a ruler. In order to create the required length of chain, remember that you should measure double that length of jump rings—e.g., for 1in (2.5cm) of chain, you need 2in (5cm) of rings.

2 Take half of the jump rings and close them by using two pairs of flat nosed pliers, manipulating the ends vertically until they meet and join perfectly. The end of the jump ring should only be closed with up and down movements and not by prying the ring open as this will distort the round shape.

3 Place the closed jump rings onto a flat firebrick. Using a clean brush, dip it in liquid flux and apply to each jump ring, paying attention to the seam area. Or, you can place the liquid flux into a small glass dish and immerse all the jump rings.

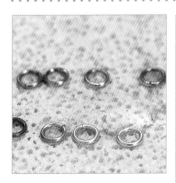

4 Set a small soft flame on the torch and allow this to brush over the jump rings, just enough to heat the pieces slightly. Do not overheat and exhaust the flux: If this occurs, apply more flux and start again.

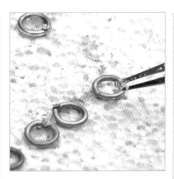

5 Place a tiny snippet of fluxed solder on top of each seam with sraight-ended stainless steel tweezers. The fluxed paillon will automatically adhere to the warmed jump ring, allowing it to be positioned securely in place.

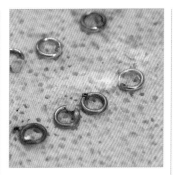

6 Turn the torch onto a small soft flame setting and heat all the jump rings gently to allow the solder to be secured and for the flux to dry slightly. Once this is achieved, set to a small precise needle neutral flame and gently heat each jump ring.

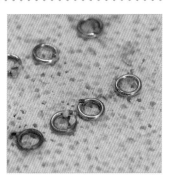

7 If the jump rings are small, be aware that they will become heated very quickly. Dull red is the optimum color of silver for solder to flow: As soon as this is reached, move onto the next jump ring until all have been soldered.

8 Once all the soldered jump rings have been cleaned in pickle solution, link them up by joining an open jump ring between two closed jump rings. Close with flat nosed pliers and continue until the chain has been created.

9 Lay the chain on a firebrick and flux the open jump rings with liquid flux. Position the unsoldered jump rings away from the closed jump ring seams, not touching and in danger of being soldered. Use reverse-action tweezers to hold the jump rings in place, if necessary. Place a small snippet of solder on the seams of a couple of jump rings.

10 Using a small soft flame, heat gently until the flux has stopped expanding. Then, adjust the torch to create a small neutral needle flame to heat each jump ring. After each successful solder join, move onto the next jump ring and repeat the process until the chain is completely soldered.

11 Any excess solder can be removed gently with emery paper. Avoid using files as these can remove too much metal and cause the jump rings to become misshapen. Once the chain has been assembled and soldered, the cleaning process can be carried out easily in a tumble polisher or with polishing mops. All polishing processes will work-harden and finish the chain off.

Once the chain has been soldered and finished, it can be applied to other jewelry parts by soldering or by linking chains together.

Soldering Tubing

TOOLS AND MATERIALS

* Pre-formed tube from flat silver sheet
* Piercing saw and saw blade
* Binding wire
* Borax cone, dish, and brush
* Hard solder strip
* Rectangular needle file and emery paper
* Round draw plate
* Pliers
* Hand vise

SKILL LEVEL 💍 💍

Tubing can perform a variety of functions in jewelry making, from hinges and bezels to end caps. Being able to produce tubing allows a jeweler to create the exact diameter and wall thickness required.

Having a selection of ready-made tubing on hand is invaluable, and you will find a number of reasons call for its use. Tubing can give the illusion of being chunky and heavy but have the advantage of being lightweight. Therefore, certain large jewelry pieces can be made from hollow tubing to reduce the weight and cost of the metal. There are jewelry designers who create stunning pieces made predominantly from formed and shaped tubes.

Tubes can also be extremely useful for making hinges or for capping off a non-metal material such as leather or synthetic cords in bracelets or torques. They can also be practical for the construction of clasps, for rivets, to create beads, and in pendant bales.

Tip

If binding wire becomes soldered to the piece, hold the wire with pliers as close to the join as possible and pull with sharp force. Any marks can be removed with files and emery paper.

Tube Making Guidelines

• During construction of the tube, check the metal sheet you work with has been cut straight and uniform. Any uneven sides will mean the formed piece will not align to make a straight tube.

• If you need to draw the tubing down in size, a drawing dog should be applied to allow the piece to be held and pulled through a draw plate.

• When tube is to be applied to another piece and the join has to be hidden, adding a few small marks or nicks to the seam area allows the jeweler to instantly locate the solder join.

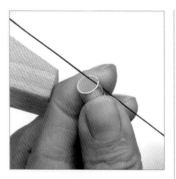

1 Taking a formed piece of tube, run a saw blade down the entire length of the seam to ensure the sides meet together perfectly.

2 Formed pieces like tubes have a tendency to spring apart, causing the join or seam to disconnect. To pull the two sides together, wrap binding wire around the tube at the top and bottom, securing it with twists. Make kinks in the wire to allow for the tube's expansion during heating.

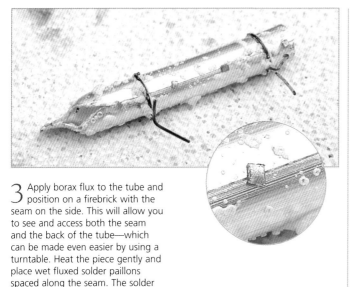

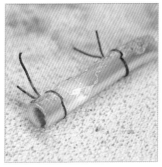

3 Apply borax flux to the tube and position on a firebrick with the seam on the side. This will allow you to see and access both the seam and the back of the tube—which can be made even easier by using a turntable. Heat the piece gently and place wet fluxed solder paillons spaced along the seam. The solder pieces will adhere and secure to the seam with low risk of falling off.

4 Heat the tube with a gentle flame, along the opposite side from the seam. As the piece starts to heat from here, the metal will expand, pushing the seam tighter together.

5 Circle the flame around the entire tube. As the tube starts to turn dull red and solder runs, direct the solder along the seam with the flame. If there is a shortage of solder, apply more pre-cut pieces from the flux dish. However, beware that excess solder can overflood and change the shape of the tube.

6 When solder has flowed successfully along the full length of the seam, withdraw the heat and allow the tube to cool. Remove the binding wire, place the tube in pickle solution, and then under clean running water, paying particular attention to the inside to remove any excess pickle. Clean any excess solder with a file and emery paper.

7 Take the tubing down one size on a draw plate to neaten it up, re-shape if it has become distorted, and to work-harden. Use pliers and a hand vise to assist you.

8 Remove the drawing dog (excess end part of tube, where the pliers gripped to pull through the draw plate) with a piercing saw. Never cut with snips as this will distort the tubing and produce an uneven end.

Once both ends of the tube have been filed and cleaned, the piece is complete. It can now be polished or applied to another component.

Tip

To avoid wasting metal if making gold tubing, add a silver wire end instead of a gold drawing dog end.

End view

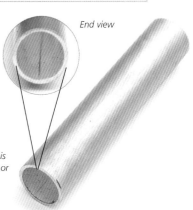

TOOLS AND MATERIALS

* Silver sheet
* Liquid flux and clean brush
* Hard silver solder
* Emery paper
* Silver square wire
* Ring mandrel
* Rawhide mallet
* Emery paper
* Borax cone, dish, and brush
* Piercing saw

SKILL LEVEL ⚭ ⚭

Multiple Solder Joins

When a piece is constructed with multiple solder joins, the key consideration is which parts should be soldered first. This allows you to establish the hardness and grades of solder to use.

If a piece of jewelry is made from a large main component and smaller applied pieces, it is wise to use the hardest solder for the large part and then work down in hardness. If you solder several joins with the same hardness of solder, keep the heat away from the solder joins you do not wish to move. If unwanted solder joins are opened, it will weaken, or even collapse the piece.

The melting temperature of solder increases every time it is heated and melted. This allows a jeweler to use the same hardness of solder in a multi-solder-join piece, only using medium solder for the final solder join. It is best to apply hard solder to as many solder joins as possible as this allows you to use lower-melting-temperature solder only for situations that really require it. For

example, joins near an area that has the risk of parts unsoldering at high temperatures. Remember that once a lower-melting-point solder has been applied, you cannot reverse it.

Easy solder is rarely used, predominantly only applied in emergency solder joins where heating to a higher temperature may risk the piece collapsing, or in repairs where the jeweler does not know the solder grade history of the piece.

When soldering many joins, the use of solder inhibitors can be considered (see pages 48–49). This can be useful for stopping a solder join from flowing into an area you do not wish, stopping previous solder joins from opening, and preventing solder from running into an area that requires movement, such as a brooch fitting.

POPPY HEAD POD RING

SUZANNE POTTER

This open wire constructed ring has been fabricated and multi-soldered together. A total of 13 solder joins have been carefully planned and set up, and hard solder used throughout in order to achieve an even color on all joins. Thorough planning prevents the various parts from collapsing during the soldering process.

1 Place four small discs of silver sheet onto a firebrick. With a clean paintbrush, apply liquid flux onto the discs. Liquid flux is ideal for small pieces as it does not expand and is easy to apply without causing pieces to move unnecessarily.

2 After applying one small snippet of hard silver solder onto each of the small discs using tweezers, sweat solder (see pages 52–53). Use a small flame to allow a clear view and to avoid the piece blowing away. Quench, pickle, and clean any excess solder with emery paper.

3 Coat liquid flux onto the back silver plate and the small discs. Position the discs on the back plate and use a medium-sized neutral flame to concentrate on the back sheet. As it starts to change to dull red, bring the flame onto the four discs. As the solder runs, remove the heat.

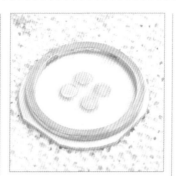

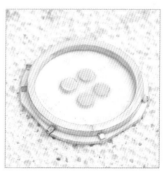

4 Shape the outer frame of square wire on a ring mandrel with a rawhide mallet. As the wire is quite pliable, use your hands to manipulate the ends until they fit tightly together. Apply liquid or borax flux and a small piece of hard silver solder on the top of the seam. Heat with a small neutral flame, first circling the entire piece and then the seam area. The solder should flow quickly. Remove the heat.

5 After allowing the piece to cool until no longer glowing, quench in water and apply the piece to pickle solution. Then, clean and re-shape it round before sanding in a figure eight on emery paper. This will flatten the base and create the optimum surface for soldering.

6 Using borax cone flux (as there is less risk of movement with this heavier-weight frame), coat the back sheet with soldered discs and the frame. Position the frame in place, central to the back plate and the soldered discs. The coating of flux on the entire piece prevents the build-up of excess fire-stain and will give previous joins a stable environment to re-flow.

7 Place small paillons of hard solder on the outside of the frame. Keeping the solder on the outer rather than the internal edge will give easier access for the cleaning of any possible excess solder and the solder seam.

8 Heat the back plate with a neutral medium flame before circling around the frame. When solder begins to run, direct the flame around the join, guiding solder along the seam. Once the solder has run smoothly around, remove the heat and allow the piece to cool for at least a minute, until the metal is no longer glowing.

9 Place the piece in pickle solution, clean in running water, and dry off. The excess metal around the frame can be removed carefully with a piercing saw. Take the saw as close in as possible but leave the slightest edge to allow solder to flow during future solder steps.

Tip

When soldering a piece with multiple joins, it is advisable to coat previous joins in flux to allow the solder to reflow to a clean area if it begins to melt. However, as solder only flows to clean areas, not applying flux to previous joins can actually help by preventing previous joins from re-flowing unnecessarily. Knowing when to apply or withhold flux on a certain piece is a valuable soldering technique that will become second nature as you practice and grow in confidence.

If you like, a brooch finding can be soldered to the back with medium silver solder. Findings should always be applied as the final solder join. Once the final join is complete, the slight edge can be filed and removed completely, prior to finishing and polishing.

TOOLS AND MATERIALS

* Silver sheet
* Ruler
* Engineer's set square
* Large flat file
* A selection of needle files
* Dividers
* Scribe
* Hand drill
* Piercing saw
* Double-sided tape
* Wooden board
* Stitching tool
* Borax cone, dish, and brush
* Hard silver solder

SKILL LEVEL 💍 💍

Using Stitches

Stitches are small, barely visible hooks that position and hold parts securely to a base, creating stability and preventing movement between the joins during soldering. They are very helpful for jewelry-making.

lthough stitches are more frequently used for silversmith pieces, when applied to jewelry they offer a quick and effective method of creating anchor points to which parts can be placed and attached. A good example of stitch use is the positioning of a bezel within a container or a stone setting that is leveled above the base of the piece. The stitches offer stable support and prevent movement during soldering, allowing the piece to be precisely soldered to the desired location.

In addition, stitches are helpful for positioning parts that require squaring or centralizing to a base plate—for instance, a square frame within a square section.

Stitching Guidelines

* Check measurements prior to stitching.

* Stitching tool must be sharp and in good working condition to safeguard precise marking.

* Ensure you are in a comfortable position and have good control of the tool. Standing is often a position that works more effectively, as your body will have more control and force to create the stitches.

* After each stitch mark, position pieces together to check accuracy prior to soldering.

ORB FRAME BROOCH

WING MUN DEVENNEY

Stitches are created at solder points and positioned into place. During soldering, stitches hold the pieces together and stop movement, allowing you to precisely place or center pieces. They are not visible on the finished part.

1 Measure two square pieces of silver sheet, 1¾ x 1¾ in (35 x 35mm) and 1 x 1 in (27 x 27mm). After measuring and piercing, use an engineer's set square and a large flat file to true the edges. This will ensure both pieces are squared and have right angles.

2 Once both parts have been accurately filed, take the smaller square piece and, using dividers, measure ⅛ in (3mm) from the edge. By aligning the outer leg of the divider on the four edges of the square, the inner leg will score an accurate square internal frame.

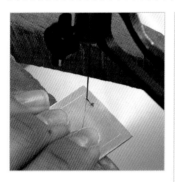

3 Mark with the scribe inside the internal frame and drill a hole for inserting the saw blade. Pierce the internal frame, allowing the saw blade to follow just inside the frame to ensure cutting of the frame is not too big.

4 File the internal frame using a rectangular needle file, again using an engineer's set-square to ensure correct right angles and straight lines are achieved. Corners of the internal frame can be filed with a small square or triangular file to produce accurate and sharp right angles.

5 On the larger square piece, using dividers, mark a ⅛ in (3mm) guideline for the stitches on all four sides. Do not place excessive force on the dividers as only fine visible lines are required.

6 Place double-sided tape on the large square section and apply to a board for support. The board, along with the larger silver square piece, should be positioned on a strong surface that is at a comfortable level for the stitching to take place.

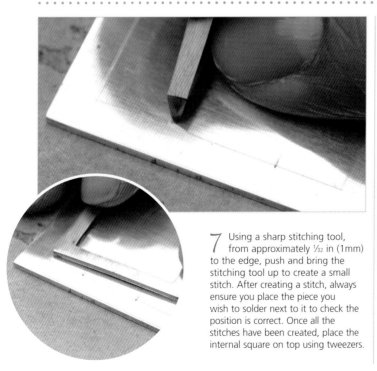

7 Using a sharp stitching tool, from approximately ¹⁄₃₂ in (1mm) to the edge, push and bring the stitching tool up to create a small stitch. After creating a stitch, always ensure you place the piece you wish to solder next to it to check the position is correct. Once all the stitches have been created, place the internal square on top using tweezers.

8 Place on a firebrick, flux, and place the solder. Here, solder paillons have been placed on the inside edge as the internal area was to be pierced away removing any visible melted solder (see bottom right). If the internal area was to be left, solder would have been placed on the outside edge where marks are easier to access and remove. If setting a stone, or internal parts are to be placed next to the join, then the solder should also be placed on the outer edge to avoid flooding this space.

9 Using a blow torch, distribute even heat with a medium-sized neutral flame onto the back piece. As the base piece is larger, it will take longer to heat, so focus the flame on this before moving around the internal frame. Once you see the solder running, direct the flow with the flame, guiding it along the seam. Remove the heat and leave to cool before placing into pickle solution. Do not quench the piece to avoid distortion.

Soldering Wire

Understanding the principles of soldering wire, be it to another wire piece or to a heavier back section, teaches the jeweler the basics of establishing heat balance between two gauges of metal.

Wire is often used for finishing pieces, be it in an earring post, bracelet clasp, brooch pin fitting, or chain-making. For this reason alone, learning to solder wire is a must for any jeweler. Wire work and detailing can also be very pretty, and many shapes and patterns can be easily formed. With an array of wire sizes and shapes available—and wire's easy-to-manipulate properties—the jeweler can be very creative and open up endless design opportunities. Wire-constructed jewelry pieces can also offer the illusion of size but, in fact, be quite lightweight.

Learning to solder wire and smaller pieces to larger bases can be tricky, especially trying to avoid melting the wire, which is finer. To do so successfully, the larger piece has to be heated to an optimum temperature before the flame is applied to the finer piece/s. Always bear in mind that solder runs into heat, so both pieces must reach the solder melting temperature at the same time. Applying heat onto the wire too early will melt the piece before the solder is ready to flow.

SYMBIOSIS NECKPIECE

ABIGAIL STRADLING

The key feature of this wire and glass neckpiece consists of fine wire soldered to heavier weight tube. The heat has been balanced to allow solder to flow without melting the fine wire.

1 Taking a piece of shaped wire, flux the complete piece, paying particular attention to the solder area. Place the wire on a firebrick and hold upright with reverse-action tweezers. Hold the tweezers at the far end of the piece, to avoid drawing heat away from the solder area.

2 Using stainless steel tweezers, apply a paillon of hard silver solder at the join. As the join is small, use a small amount. The removal of excess solder near delicate areas can be difficult and cause misshaping.

3 Use a small neutral flame to heat along the entire piece, then focus on the upper section where the seam is. As the flux becomes glassy and the wire turns dull red, the solder will run. The wire will heat quickly, so withdraw the heat as soon as solder runs to avoid melting. Cool, quench, and immerse in pickle solution.

4 After removing from pickle solution, wash in water and sand the end and the base of the curved section along emery paper. This will create a flat platform on both ends, allowing the piece to sit flush with the base. Once sanding is complete, clean with water to get rid of any dust particles.

5 Coat the base sheet and the wire with flux, paying close attention to the previous solder join. Position the wire and hold in place with reverse-action tweezers. Place a small piece of solder at both solder seams.

6 Heat gently at first, to dry the solder and allow the paillon to stick to the surface of the seams. Once the flux is dry, take the flame to the base piece. As this is the heavier weight, it will take longer to heat. When the base starts to change to dull red, direct the flame to the wire; this will become heated quickly.

7 Concentrate on one join first, circling the flame on both the base and the wire seam area. This will allow the two areas to maintain a consistent heat. As soon as the solder flows, move the torch to the next join. Circle the join. Again, the solder should flow quickly and, as it does, remove the heat immediately to avoid melting the wire.

8 Once soldering is complete, let the piece cool before placing it in pickle solution. Allow the piece to cool and stop glowing before quenching, as placing in water too quickly can cause distortion.

9 When the piece has been removed from pickle solution and washed, any excess solder can be removed carefully with emery paper. If only small quantities of solder were applied, there should be minimal cleaning required. Your piece can now be finished and polished.

Additional parts can be further applied and soldered. Remember, always solder heavier weight components together first before applying fine details.

GOLD AND SILVER BROOCH WITH ROSE-CUT DIAMONDS

MARK NUELL

Combining 22kt yellow gold and silver, the main body of this piece is press-formed silver with a gold frame soldered around the edge. The gold settings were soldered in place with hard silver solder and heat applied from the back of the piece, and the pebble features domed and sweat soldered in place.

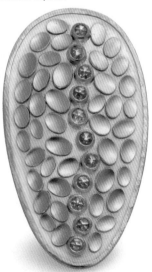

Soldering Gold and Silver Together

Using two contrasting colors of metal works very well visually. However, care has to be taken when soldering silver and gold because of gold's higher melting temperature.

Adding gold to a silver piece can instantly increase its value. The higher the karat of gold used, the more prominent the contrast of the two metals will be. Soldering of gold is similar to that of silver. As with silver, the pieces you wish to solder have to be well fitted, clean, and fluxed. Borax mixed with water produces an efficient flux for gold, but there are also a wide selection of good liquid fluxes for sale, which also work well with higher temperature metals and solders, such as gold.

When working with gold, just as when soldering silver, if there is more than one join, start with the hardest of solders and work your way down. Prior to soldering, select the right solder for the piece, matching the color and karat. To make it easier to flow and avoid the piece melting, ensure the gold solder is thinner than the piece you wish to solder. You can flatten it by running the solder stripe through a wire rolling mill or using a flat planishing hammer against a flat stake. Unlike with silver, however, with gold you do not need to heat the entire piece but can concentrate on and around the area of the seam and solder.

Because of silver's lower melting point, when soldering gold and silver together, it is best to use hard silver solder or apply easy gold. This will prevent the risk of overheating and melting the silver. In addition, it is much more cost-effective to use silver solder instead of gold, and the use of silver solder does not affect the look or workings of the piece.

Although there is a more dramatic color difference between silver and higher-karat gold than lower-value gold, there is obviously a cost factor. Silver and 9kt gold can work well together at a lower cost. However, due to the 9kt gold alloys, it can have a tendency to fuse into, rather than solder onto, the silver. To avoid this problem, bring heat from behind the piece rather than placing direct heat from the top.

1 Bend and shape a heart from the 9kt yellow gold with pliers. Fit the ends so the two meet together well. The wire at one end must have a flat plane to lie flush against the connecting side of the opposite end of wire.

2 Place the piece on a firebrick and paint with liquid flux, paying close attention to the join. For fine precious-metal soldering such as gold, liquid flux offers lower risk of parts movement compared to expandable borax flux.

3 Carefully place a small snippet of 9kt hard gold solder on the seam, touching both parts of metal. Heat the entire area with a small gentle neutral flame. Then focus on the join. Due to the fineness of the gold, it will become hot and solder will flow very quickly.

4 Once the solder has run, remove the heat immediately to avoid melting the gold. Leave the piece to cool before quenching and immersing in pickle solution. Remove, dry, and clean any excess solder with emery paper.

5 Rest the silver heart on a platform built with two firebricks on either side, bridged with a section of enamel wire mesh. Place the gold heart on top of the silver piece and paint the surface of the silver back plate and the gold heart with liquid flux.

6 Place small paillons of hard silver solder on the outside edge of the heart. This will allow easier access to remove any excess solder or marks.

7 With a medium-sized gentle flame, heat the piece from beneath the wire mesh. Allow even heat dispersion by circling the flame below.

8 As the solder starts to melt, ensure there is even solder flow around the entire edge of the heart. Once this has been achieved, remove heat and allow the piece to cool for at least a minute, until no longer glowing. Quench, pickle, and wash. Check the solder join and remove any excess solder with appropriately shaped files or emery paper.

By soldering a wire post onto the back, and creating a mirror-image piece to match, this piece could easily become an earring.

TOOLS AND MATERIALS
* Flat file
* Cast silver object
* Flat silver sheet
* Coarse emery paper
* Burnisher
* Borax cone, dish, and brush
* Hard silver solder

SKILL LEVEL 💍 💍

Soldering Cast Pieces

Cast parts can be heavy and extremely porous, making soldering difficult. The irregular shapes and forms that are created by casting can also prove difficult in the soldering set-up.

There are often occasions when the body of a piece cannot be constructed by fabrication alone. Cast items can offer a variety of shapes and forms, in addition to allowing the production of multiple identical pieces. However, the porosity of cast pieces not only inhibits successful soldering but can be costly, as the solder is consumed by the cast component. Recent casting techniques have improved and progressed enormously, allowing high-quality castings to be achieved. However, casting parts at home by using cuttlefish bone, charcoal, or Red Oil Sand can still produce slightly porous components, making further development and solder work difficult.

In a commercial environment, for the sake of time-efficiency and cost-effectiveness, the main body of a piece is often made by stamp or cast procedure and then findings or finishing parts are soldered on at the final stage. To do so successfully, an ideal soldering area must be created. For example, if the cast component is later to be fitted with cufflink findings, it should be cast with a flat platform area where the two can join neatly together. Study how the two surfaces will lie and join together; how the cast piece can be worked on to achieve a good fit and optimum soldering surface; and which tools and equipment can assist in the soldering process.

LTD EDITION PURPLE AND GOLD RING

JANE GOWANS

The use of casting can open up exciting design and production possibilities This ring has been made from partially cast and fabricated parts but, interestingly, the cast component was originally constructed by soldering. This illustrates the diversity that soldering can offer. Casting the main component allows many identical pieces to be produced and allows further soldering to be carried out easily and relatively risk-free.

1 Using a flat file, fit the base of the cast piece to the flat silver sheet. Also ensure the silver sheet is as flat as possible: If required, tap gently against a flat plate or bench block with a rawhide mallet

2 Once the parts fit well together, sand the base of the cast part against coarse emery paper in a figure eight motion. This will create a flat top edge that will fit perfectly against the flat silver sheet.

3 Work a burnisher across the solder area. Draw the burnisher away from yourself and at an angle to the right. Continue this action until the surface is polished. This repeated action will close off any porosity pit holes, thus reducing the risk of excess solder bleeding into the piece during soldering.

4 Coat the cast piece in flux, paying close attention to the base surface, and place on a firebrick. Place paillons of hard silver solder close to the edges and in the center of the piece. Bear in mind that sweat soldering works best when the solder is close to the edge.

5 Heat with a medium-sized flame until the solder flows over the surface. Remove the heat and allow the piece to cool before quenching in cool water and immersing in pickle solution.

6 When the piece has been washed and dried, remove any excess solder with a flat file or coarse emery paper. File down until the globules of solder are flattened.

7 Paint flux onto the base sheet and place onto a firebrick. Coat the cast piece in flux and flip it over so that the solder is facing downward onto the silver sheet.

8 Using a medium-sized flame, heat the cast piece first. Once the cast part starts to heat, move the torch around the base sheet, which will allow both to reach an optimum temperature for solder to flow. Once solder has run successfully around the required areas, remove the heat and allow the piece to cool for at least a minute, until no longer glowing, before quenching in water and placing in pickle solution.

The burnishing action produces a secure surface for the solder to flow and prevents excess solder from developing. Additionally, sweat soldering this multi-rounded shape creates a clean solder join which otherwise would have been difficult to access if excess solder had developed from another soldering technique.

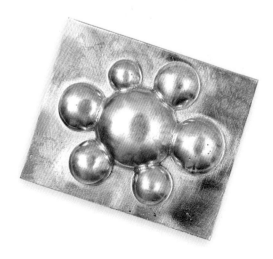

Stick Feed Soldering

This is an excellent technique for pieces with areas that require a large amount of solder, for lengthy solder channels, or for areas where snippets of solder are difficult to place.

This solder technique allows sufficient amounts of solder to flow easily into lengthy or awkward channels and avoids any solder gaps. It is often used for larger silversmith pieces, but it can be extremely useful for any jewelry items with lengthy seams. Stick feeding allows solder flow to be drawn from one piece of solder along a channel. It takes quite a bit of practice, but once the technique is perfected, the jeweler can confidently solder lengthy joins without the time-consuming and often impossible placement of paillons.

Mastered correctly, stick feed soldering can create a smooth and clean solder join. However, carried out incorrectly, it can produce a messy seam with excess globules and drops of solder. This can make the cleaning process difficult and time-consuming.

The secret to successful stick feed soldering is to apply the heat past the solder so the solder flows into the heated area. Therefore, it is best to hold the length of solder at the beginning of the seam and position the heat along the seam after the solder. Once the metals are at the optimum temperature, guide the solder along the seam with the flame. Do not place the heat directly onto the solder as this will inevitably melt it, causing drops of molten solder on the surface.

Stick Feed Soldering Guidelines

• Make sure the length of solder is straight, clean, and fluxed—but most importantly it should be sufficiently long. Allow extra length for the piece to be held securely.

• The channel for stick soldering should be no different from that for paillon soldering: It should be clean and a tight fit. The purpose of stick soldering is not to flood gaps or areas where solder has failed to run, but to allow solder to flow along a lengthy or difficult-to-reach join.

1 Anneal the narrower strip of silver (see page 41) and then form and shape into a curve on a bangle stake. As the piece will be quite soft, it can be easily manipulated by hand without using a mallet.

2 Place the piece against the bench-peg for support and, using a large flat file, level the edge surface. Check against the flat silver strip to ensure the pieces fit well together.

3 Sand the surface of the flat strip and the bottom edge of the curved strip with emery paper, making sure you have an ideal surface for the solder to flow.

4 With a paintbrush, apply flux to the base piece and place onto a firebrick. Flux the curved strip, paying particular attention to the base edge, before positioning onto the flat strip.

5 Taking a strip of hard silver solder, cut a thin length from the edge with sharp shears. As you cut, the thin piece is likely to curve back onto itself: To make it usable, straighten with flat pliers.

6 Hold the thin length of solder on reverse-action tweezers and paint with flux. Holding the torch with one hand, place the tweezers with solder in the opposite hand, ready to position.

7 Set the torch to a medium-sized neutral flame and heat the back plate before delivering heat around the curved piece. The piece will start to heat up and flux will start to expand. As the piece changes color, bring the solder in, allowing it to touch the corner of the two pieces.

8 Place the flame in front of the solder and, as it starts to flow to the heat, continue to move the flame along the seam, drawing the solder along. Do not place the flame directly onto the solder as it will melt into globules.

9 Once the piece has been allowed to cool, quench and place in pickle solution. This technique should produce a clean solder seam, but if you find excess solder at the start of the join, clean with emery paper.

This technique is ideal for curved seams which would otherwise be difficult to access and clean. The only excess solder which requires removal can be seen here at the start of the join and can be easily accessed with coarse emery paper or needle files.

TOOLS AND MATERIALS
* Two silver sheets, one smaller and plain and one larger and pre-textured
* Borax cone, dish, and brush
* Hard silver solder
* Emery paper
* Rouge powder, container, water, and clean brush

SKILL LEVEL ○

GREEN LEAF RING
CHRIS AND JOY POUPAZIS

The texture on this ring adds depth to the piece and gives a strong contrast between the matte texture and the highly polished wire on top. The shaped wire is sweat soldered onto the textured surface to avoid spillage of excess solder. Sweat soldering the three layers when the parts are flat allows even and precise sweat soldering to occur between each.

Soldering onto a Textured Surface

Surface texture and decorations are great methods of enhancing a piece of jewelry, but extra care must be taken while soldering to avoid solder flowing into the patterns.

When solder and textured metals are involved, it is best to think about the flow of solder and how to prevent it running into unwanted areas. Whether the solution is a wall constructed from a setting or painting the surface texture with solder inhibitor, bear this in mind during the design process. Ultimately, the safest option is to simply cut the textured pattern and apply it on top of your piece, or the pattern can be inlaid into a piece and soldered from the back.

If the component being soldered onto the textured surface is a rub-over stone setting, it is wise to place the solder on the inside of the setting. Of course, excess solder should not be used as it could make the setting too small or create a raised solder join, which would prevent the stone from sitting flush or flat.

A good method to follow to avoid running solder into a textured sheet when applying a frame is to make the piece slightly bigger than required and apply the solder onto the outside of the frame. Once soldered, pierce away the additional metal on the outside of the frame.

Another useful technique for soldering onto a textured surface is to sweat solder (see pages 52–53) onto the piece that is applied on top of the texture. This allows the solder to remain underneath the piece rather than applying to the edges of the two pieces, which would run more risk of solder running into the texture.

1 Check the small silver piece sits flush on top of the textured back sheet. Paint the small piece with borax flux and place small snippets of hard silver solder. If the base piece is larger than the piece you wish to sweat solder on top, then the paillons should be placed close to the edges of the smaller piece to ensure the solder will be drawn close to the seam.

2 Using a small neutral flame, heat the small piece until the solder runs. Once the solder has flowed, remove the heat. Allow the piece to cool down before placing in pickle solution and then clean water.

3 Remove any excess solder by sanding on a sheet of emery paper. This will not only eliminate excess solder but also allow the surface to be as flat and sit as flush as possible on the base plate. After sanding, clean off dust and apply flux to the surface, then apply the solder snippets.

4 Paint flux onto the central area of the textured piece, making sure the application is kept within this space. Flux will allow solder to flow and we do not want any solder to escape from the central area.

Tip

If you wish to be more accurate, position the smaller piece in the correct place on the textured part. Use a scribe and lightly mark the exact location by working around the edge of the smaller piece. Once you remove this the marks will be visible and you can paint flux exactly into this box.

5 With a clean paintbrush, carefully apply a coating of rouge powder mixed with water to the outer area of the textured piece. Allow a slight gap between the flux and the rouge to avoid the two mixing together. If this happens, clean the piece with soapy water and a soft hand brush before starting again.

6 Paint flux onto the base surface of the smaller piece, where the solder is.

7 Place the textured piece onto a firebrick and then position the pre-sweat-soldered piece carefully in the center. Ensure the piece does not touch the rouge as this will prevent solder flowing.

8 Start by heating the base textured sheet as it is larger and will take longer to heat. Then bring the flame onto the un-textured piece, moving the flame continuously to get an even distribution of heat. As the base piece is covered with rouge, it will be more difficult to recognize its color change, so use the top piece as a guide. As this piece turns dull red, direct the flame along the seams to lead the flow of solder.

9 Once solder has run all along the square join, withdraw the heat, cool, wash off the rouge paint, and place in pickle solution. If excess solder has run, gently clean with emery paper.

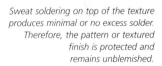

Sweat soldering on top of the texture produces minimal or no excess solder. Therefore, the pattern or textured finish is protected and remains unblemished.

TOOLS AND MATERIALS

* Silver sheet for creating domes and applied detail
* Scribe
* Dome block and punches
* Rawhide mallet
* Emery paper
* Hand drill
* Piercing saw
* Selection of needle files
* Borax cone, dish, and brush
* Hard silver solder
* Binding wire
* Round nosed pliers

SKILL LEVEL 💍💍

Soldering a Hollow Form

Creating a piece of jewelry from a hollow form can allow it to be large and look weighty, while actually being lightweight, comfortable to wear, and cost-effective to make.

A hollow construction can benefit jewelry pieces such as heavy-look rings, large beads, sizeable earrings, and grand pendants and neckpieces. In a commercial environment, many pieces are manufactured hollow to reduce the cost of the metal and improve wearability. Whenever you are designing a piece, ask yourself if it will be too heavy to wear, and whether a hollow construction would help.

All sorts of shapes and sizes of metal forms can be fabricated and soldered together to create a hollow form but, when doing so, two important factors have to be considered. The first is to make sure the surface areas soldered together are as large as possible to allow a strong bond. The second is to always create an air hole to allow air to escape during the soldering process. Without this, the trapped air will expand and the piece may as well, not just ruining the jewelry but also posing great danger to the jeweler.

To create a large and flush surface area for solder, it is best to emery the joins down to a flat plane. The air hole can be a simple, small, drilled hole that is discreetly hidden within the design of the piece, be it by a stone setting or within a pierced pattern or shape that is reflective of the design.

1 Use two discs of silver sheet, one with a pre-sweat-soldered diamond applied detail (see pages 52–53), and the other plain. Draw a smaller matching diamond shape onto the plain disc with a scribe. Anneal both discs and allow to cool before placing in pickle solution.

2 Place the annealed, unsoldered disc into a doming block with the scribed diamond on the underside. Form the dome using a doming punch and rawhide mallet. Repeat with the disc with the pre-soldered diamond, again by placing the diamond shape on the base.

3 Using coarse emery paper, sand the bases of the two domes in a figure eight manner until flat. This will not only make the edges of the two domes meet flush, but also increase the surface area for soldering. After sanding, check the fit of the two domes, base to base.

4 Drill a hole in the center of the scribed dome, then pierce the diamond shape carefully with a piercing saw. Keep the saw blade inside the scribed lines to ensure you do not remove any excess metal.

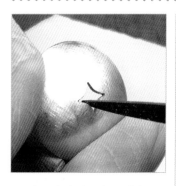

5 File and tidy the edges of the pierced diamond shape with a needle file. To get into the corners, a triangular file is ideal, as it will not misshape or remove too much of the metal.

6 Flux the edge of the pierced dome and, on a firebrick, apply slight heat from a neutral flame. Use tweezers to apply small paillons of hard silver solder which will now adhere to this heated narrow platform area.

7 Heat with a medium-sized neutral flame and allow the solder to run. Remove the heat and allow to cool before cleaning in pickle solution and water. Sand down any excess or lumps of solder with emery paper or files.

8 Flux both domes on their edges and outer surfaces to avoid excess build-up of fire-stain. Ensure that flux is applied to the previously soldered diamond shape to allow the solder to re-flow when heated again.

9 Use binding wire to secure the two pieces together to form the hollow shape and add notches with round nosed pliers. This will allow room for the silver to expand without the wire marking the metal.

10 Heat with a medium-sized neutral flame, concentrating on both domes until they start to turn dull red, then circle the flame round the seam to allow the solder to run completely around.

11 Allow the piece to cool before removing the binding wire. If you find any part of the wire has become soldered, then hold close to the join with pliers and give a short, sharp pull to pry it apart.

12 After placing in pickle solution and washing with water, clean any excess solder with files and emery papers.

Tip

After soldering a hollow form, it is vital to remove all traces of acidic pickle solution (which will eat into the solder and metal) using running water. For items with a very small drill hole, place in a solution of water and bicarbonate of soda, and boil for 5–10 minutes. Any water inside can be dried with a blow dryer on a low setting.

This piece can be cleaned and polished, or applied to another piece. Further soldering can be achieved safely as long as the air hole remains unblocked and uncovered.

Scored and Folded Chamfered Joins

Chamfered joins are much stronger than butt joins due to the increased soldering surface area. They create sharp edges and clean lines, making them a must for any boxlike construction.

TOOLS AND MATERIALS

* Silver sheet
* Double-sided tape
* Wooden block
* Dividers
* Metal ruler
* Scoring tool
* Parallel flat nosed pliers
* Binding wire
* Borax cone, dish, and brush
* Hard silver solder
* Round nose pliers
* Rectangular emery stick

SKILL LEVEL ⬡ ⬡

Chamfered Join Guidelines

• Once the scoring and folding are completed, keep the piece as still as possible to prevent the metal from splitting and breaking off entirely. Solder as quickly as possible.

• To fold larger pieces, use a hand vise, which will offer a more stable and stronger support. Always cover with protectors to prevent the vise from marking the metal.

Chamfered joins created from scored and folded metal allow the solder seams to be entirely concealed inside the construction. This method also offers a very stable construction for soldering. Scoring and folding are useful for creating any piece of jewelry that requires precise, sharp, straight lines, such as hollow containers, box clasps, square or rectangular rub-over settings, and corner frames.

The first step is to score the metal, making sure that the lines you cut into the metal are accurate and perfectly straight. Measure carefully using a set square and a metal ruler as a guide, then score using a sharp tool and a steady hand. The metal is then folded at a 90-degree angle. Scoring and folding of metals can be carried out on both sheet and wire forms. If working with wire, the removal of metal should be performed with square and triangular files.

1 Taking the silver sheet, place double-sided tape onto the back and apply to a wooden block to allow the piece to be secured and easily held down for the scoring process. This will prevent the piece from slipping away from your hand, causing inaccurate scores.

2 Using dividers held against the edge of the sheet, mark a line down the metal. Repeat with the other side so you have two parallel guidelines to follow. The divider width is determined by how wide you wish the fold to be.

3 Position a metal ruler on one line and, using a scoring tool, follow the side of the ruler. Lean on the line lightly for the first couple of scores to allow the scored line to be accurate. Once an accurate, defined line has been created, follow this with the scoring tool, using firm pressure to remove metal.

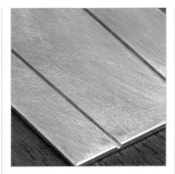

4 Continue, using the same pressure along the line to avoid removing uneven quantities of metal. Inconsistent metal removal can affect the bend of the metal. Repeat the scoring until a "V"-shaped groove is approximately half the depth of the metal thickness.

5 Repeat the process for the second line. Check both scored lines have the same depth of metal removed so the angles of the folds will be identical.

6 Carefully remove the piece from the board and take away the double-sided tape. As this piece is small, the bending can be carried out by hand with a pair of pliers. Use the bench-peg to steady and push against.

7 When both sides have been folded upright and are aligned parallel with each other, fix the piece securely with binding wire using round nose pliers. This will stop the sides from moving and falling during the heating and soldering process. Remember to add a few notches to the binding wire to allow for expansion of the silver.

8 Place onto a firebrick. Paint flux onto the piece, concentrating on both seams. Use tweezers to dot solder paillons along the seams. Always bear in mind that small amounts of solder can travel great distances so you should take care not to be excessive.

9 Using a medium-sized neutral flame, heat the entire piece. As the piece is of substantial metal, it may take a moment to heat evenly. Once it has started to turn dull red in color, concentrate on one seam, both internally and externally. As the solder flows, guide it along with the flame. Upon completion, move to the second join and, once the solder flows, remove the heat.

10 Allow to cool for at least a minute until no longer glowing, quench in water, and place in pickle solution. If the correct amount of solder has been used, minimal cleaning is required. To remove any marks or excess solder, use a rectangular emery stick. This will allow the sharp folds to be maintained.

The scoring and removal of approximately 50 percent of the metal thickness has created perfect right angles on this piece. You can use this technique to create folds at any angle by removing more or less metal.

Soldering of Inlay

Inlaying of metals is a wonderful method for adding contrasting color, pattern, or texture to a piece. Inlay can consist of simple stripes or dots, or intricately detailed designs.

TOOLS AND MATERIALS

* ★ Piercing saw and fine blades
* ★ Silver sheet
* ★ Copper sheet (same thickness as the silver)
* ★ Selection of needle files
* ★ Scribe
* ★ Center punch
* ★ Hand drill
* ★ Emery paper
* ★ Borax cone, dish, and brush
* ★ Hard silver solder

SKILL LEVEL 💍💍

The traditional method of inlaying metals involved chiseling and cutting metal away from the surface, deep enough to tap and insert a contrasting color of metal. The pattern or shape that was removed was done at an angle so that when the new metal was tapped and forced into the recesses it remained secured. However, the type of inlay described here is not the traditional method but the "pierced inlay" or "marrying of metals" technique, which is when pierced sections of metal are replaced with metal of the same shape but in a contrasting color, and then secured by soldering.

To inlay well, you must be able to pierce well and be patient enough to fit the pieces together tightly. As with any soldering, the two edges have to fit well enough together to allow the solder to flow successfully. Check the fitting by holding the two pieces fitted together up to a light: If light passes between, the gaps are too big for soldering.

Tip

As a beginner to inlay, it is advisable to work in shapes that are easy to replicate, such as round discs or straight lines. Any shapes or patterns that are organically detailed or ornate may prove difficult to replicate and fit, making the soldering process difficult.

Tip

Always use the inlay piece as a template to mark on the base sheet. This will ensure the part you pierce away is accurate and as close a fit as possible.

INLAID RING
WILL EVANS

The yellow gold inlaid detail works well against the background of white gold. The composition of the square stones enhances the overall design. Wire and square sections were carefully inlaid into the white gold and the soldering occurred at the back of the piece before scoring and folding to form the box-like construction and attaching to the shank.

1 With a piercing saw, cut a small copper and a larger silver drop shape, then shape them with needle files. Make sure the small copper shape is filed and shaped accurately, as this will be used as the template as well as the inlay piece.

2 Place the copper piece in the center of the silver piece and draw around it with a scribe. This produces an accurate and matching outline to pierce away for the insertion of inlay.

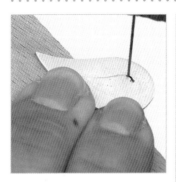

3 After creating a mark with a center punch, drill a hole for inserting a piercing saw blade. Cut carefully inside the line to ensure you do not remove too much metal.

4 File the inside of the pierced-out shape carefully, continually checking against the smaller copper piece. If necessary, file the copper inlay too. Ensure you do not over-file and make the space for fitting the copper piece too big. Take your time and check the fit after every couple of strokes with the file.

5 Once the copper shape fits snugly, with no light passing between the pieces, you are ready to solder. If there is light visible through the join, the gap is too large to allow solder to flow. Give the edges to be soldered a rub with emery paper to create clean surfaces.

6 With the copper piece inserted into the silver part, determine which side is the back and flux the internal edges where the two metals meet. Coat the top and base surfaces with flux and place on a firebrick back facing upward. Place hard silver solder paillons along the seam at the back, making sure that they touch both metals.

7 Gently heat the entire piece with a circling medium-sized neutral flame. As the two pieces start to change color to dull red, focus on the join and lead the solder along using the flame. Remove heat as soon as even solder flow is achieved.

8 After allowing the piece to cool until it is no longer glowing—at least a minute—quench in water and place in pickle solution. As solder was applied from the back, the front should have a clean solder edge—only the back should require any cleaning of excess solder. This can be carried out with emery paper or sticks.

Now the piece can be formed, shaped, or applied to other components. This mixture of copper and silver is a distinctive contrast but either of the metals could also be colored to offer a further distinction between the metals.

Investment Soldering

Investment plaster can be of great assistance in securing difficult pieces together, allowing one solder action for multiple solder points. It also opens up countless design possibilities.

Buying Investment Powder

There are a range of investment powders available from jewelry suppliers and the type used for silver casting is ideal for this technique. Make sure that you only use jewelry investment powder, as other types of plaster may not withstand the heat produced in soldering and would pose a fire risk.

Investment powder or plaster is commonly used for casting metal jewelry. However, the properties of this material also make it ideal for holding parts securely in place for soldering. The powder is mixed with water to form a liquid that can be poured into a container or mold, and parts inserted into the plaster will be held securely once the plaster sets.

The benefit of using this technique is being able to set up and position your pieces in whatever manner and position you wish. As long as the parts are sitting flush together and can be held in place with wax or modeling clay, the joining and soldering process is possible. This technique is particularly useful for the construction of basket settings and detailed wirework pieces. Or perhaps the parts you wish to join are awkwardly shaped, too small to hold with a jig, or there are many joins which would risk movement or unsoldering during the numerous soldering joins required. Bear in mind that the plaster is only there to hold the piece in place and not to force together ill-fitting parts. All parts should also be cleaned and fluxed as usual.

1 Mold the clay into a round thick disk, approximately 1¼ in (30mm) in diameter by ⅝ in (16mm) in height. Take a pre-soldered ½ in (14mm) diameter ring and press it lightly into the center of the clay, and then remove it, so leaving an indentation.

2 Place a ½ x ½ in (12 x 12mm) square template over the circle imprint and mark the four corners with a scribe. Remove the template.

3 Insert four wire pieces into each of the marked corners, pushing each in approximately two-thirds of its length. Taking a length of cardstock or paper, wrap tightly around the construction and secure the end with masking tape.

4 Mix the investment powder with water in a plastic pitcher according to the manufacturer's instructions. Pour the plaster into the casing until it is level with the top.

5 Allow the plaster to dry, again following the manufacturer's instructions. Once the plaster is dry, remove the modeling clay, which will reveal the parts for soldering. The four pieces of wire are now secured in place by the plaster.

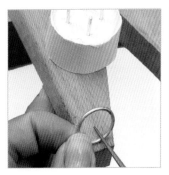

6 Taking the original round ring, file grooves at four points to match the four wires. Use a round needle file so that the round wires will fit closely with the ring. This will produce close fits and stronger solder joins.

7 Coat the upper section of the wire pieces and the ring with flux. Slide the ring onto the wire pieces, matching the shaped grooves with the position of the wires before placing onto a firebrick. Apply a small paillon of solder to each join, making sure that it touches both surfaces.

8 Using a medium-sized neutral flame, heat the pieces, starting with the individual wire pieces. As these have been embedded in plaster, they will take longer to heat. Once they start to heat, focus the heat around the ring and also the top section of each wire.

9 As the piece starts to change to dull red in color, focus the flame on each join. When solder flows, move onto the next join until all four have been successfully soldered. Allow the piece to cool before moving.

10 Lift the cooled piece with stainless steel tweezers and immerse in a container of cold water. It may bubble slightly from the internal heat within the plaster, so take care.

11 Remove the remaining plaster by hand and clean with a large brush before placing in pickle solution. If the wires are slightly off angle, tweak and straighten with pliers.

Further soldering work can be applied to this piece, but care should be taken to prevent parts from collapsing. Application of lower-melting-point solder is recommended.

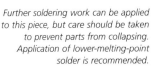

Chapter 3
Post-soldering Processes

Only after the final solder join has been completed can the cleaning and polishing processes begin. Successful solder joins require minimal treatment; however, soldering can often be unpredictable, and even in the most optimum environment with the most precise set-up and solder application, there will be occasion for even the most experienced jeweler to repair mistakes. This can be simply the removal of excess solder or the more time-consuming task of un-soldering incorrectly joined parts.

Once all soldering has been completed, correct steps and procedures must be followed to ensure the best finish is achieved on a piece. This chapter will cover each of these stages, from quenching through to the polishing or metal coloring stages. Also, detailed instructions on amending incorrectly soldered parts will be presented along with the removal of fire-stain and solder marks.

Quenching, Cooling, Cleaning

It is important to understand the procedures needed to clean off excess solder without damage to the piece. Also vital is to know how to remove the dark shadow of fire-stain.

Fixing Mistakes

Mistakes happen and even for an experienced jeweler, there will be occasions when a join gets soldered incorrectly. If that is the case, the join can be removed by reheating and disengaging.

Immerse the piece in pickle solution to remove any oxides, old flux, and dirt before applying new, clean flux. Flux the entire piece to avoid excess formation of fire-stain. If there are joins that you are worried about opening, cover them with solder inhibitor. Position the piece with the part you wish to unsolder to the top, securing the base of the piece with pins if required. Using reverse-action tweezers, hold the piece you wish to unsecure and heat with a small flame. Concentrate the flame only around the incorrectly soldered join. Wait until solder runs and pull apart by moving the tweezers. If the area requires additional support, it might be handy to use a third arm or reverse-action tweezers to hold one piece down while using your free hand and stainless steel tweezers to lift the part away. Once the pieces have been disconnected, immerse in pickle solution, then remove all traces of solder with files and emery paper before re-soldering. Take care to remove old solder to prevent it from being re-heated and possibly corroding the metal.

If the incorrectly soldered piece only requires a slight move, then while the solder is flowing use the tweezers to carefully shift it to the required position. Once you have achieved the correct positioning of the piece, remove heat, pickle, and clean any excess solder with files and emery papers. Take note that this procedure requires concentration and steady hands.

Quenching and Cooling

Typically, the first step of the post-soldering process is to quench the piece in cool water. However, there are some metals that would be damaged by quenching. For example, quenching white gold causes brittleness and risk of cracking. If you have a soldered piece that needs to remain flat, then quenching will also not be the best option as it can cause distortion.

It is important to know that the optimum heat for quenching is when the metal is no longer glowing red in color: Never immerse a metal into water when it is bright red—many metals would shatter and crack, resulting in irreversible damage.

Once metals have cooled or been quenched, they should be transferred to a pickle solution to remove all traces of flux, oxides, solder marks, and some fire-stain. Remove any binding wire or heat-insulating gels that can contaminate and cause damage to the pickle solution or other pieces.

Removal of Excess Solder

Where there is excess solder, it is best to evaluate the area before taking any tools to it. Think about the shapes around the solder and tools that will fit into the area. Incorrectly shaped tools or excess filing will remove metal and change the shape of the piece. Protecting areas with masking tape will help keep them clear of filing and emery marks. Always file with steady and controlled movements. If filing inside a ring, move the file in a curved movement, and if on a flat surface, file in one straight, swift forward glide, without moving back on yourself. Position the piece against a strong support to allow you to apply sufficient pressure.

The most useful tool is a set of small needle files. Emery papers are also essential, perhaps wrapped around rods of dowel or sticks, held in place with tape. For minute crevices, small sections of emery paper wrapped around themselves can be useful. For a faster cleaning process, abrasive and silicon wheels from a pendant motor/hand-held flexible shaft can assist greatly. Before you take a file or emery paper to your piece, ensure you place it against a stable base. Filing freehand will cause uneven removal. I find the bench peg a particularly useful platform as it allows the piece to be held in place easily and for easy access of tools.

Spots or globules of solder can be removed with flat files. Make sure the files are not angled, which can cause file marks. File using only forward swift sweeps.

To remove excess solder from the space between round wires, use a triangular file. This will allow access into the area without removing metal or distorting the curve of the wire.

In right-angled areas, such as a folded and soldered join, use square or rectangular files and emery sticks. These will protect and maintain the sharp right angle while removing any excess solder from the seam.

When working on the inside of a round shank, be it a ring or a bangle, the ideal files and tools to use are round or half round/ "D-shaped."

To use the half round and round file, instead of filing in and outward on the internal shank, push and turn the file as you move inward. If you think of the shank as a clock, with the "6 o'clock" position sitting flat against the bench peg, the file should start from the "7 o'clock" position and curve forward until it

reaches "3 o'clock." Tailor accordingly to the size of the piece. When one area of the circumference of the shank has been filed, rotate the piece to the next section to maintain an even removal of metal around the inside.

To create an even surface on the top of a ledge, such as the top and base of a ring, or even the top edge of a bezel, the best option is to file first with a large flat file. To ensure even filing, do so in forward swift movements and remember to turn the piece over and file from both angles. Once filing has created a completely flat surface, place the piece onto coarse emery paper and sand down in a figure eight motion. This will ensure the edge is completely level.

Emery papers are available in both wet and dry options, as well as various grades. For standard silver pieces, it is best to use grades 280, 400, 800, and 1000. Emery papers can be wrapped around a stick or board and held in place with double-sided tape. This will allow more pressure to be applied to the piece.

To give added strength to the emery paper, it can be wrapped around other tools, such as files. Wrap around various shapes of files and hold in place with tape before using against the piece.

Emery paper can also be folded and wrapped around itself. It can be folded into different shapes to fit around the areas you wish to sand, which is especially useful for difficult-to-access regions.

Removal of Fire-stain

Fire-stain or fire-scale occurs when metals alloyed with copper, such as silver and low-karat golds, are heated in an oxygenated environment. Cupric oxide forms and gives the surface a dark shadow. The only method of avoiding the stain is to solder in oxygen-free surroundings, which is not commonly possible for an independent jeweler. Note that light coatings of fire-stain may not require such a strenuous removal process as that described here—they may be removed by pickle solution or polishing.

To identify fire-stain, place the piece at an angle against a white background, such as a piece of paper or card. Against the white, the gray shadows of fire-stain become easily visible. As shown here, there are blotches of gray shadow across the surface of this piece.

Once the area of fire-stain has been noted, place the piece against a stable support such as the bench peg and then apply pressure from a file. If the area being worked on is small, a needle file will be sufficient. A larger area may require larger files, so adjust accordingly.

Fire-stain can also be removed by using water of Ayr stone. To use, immerse the stone in clean water and then rub onto the area in a circular motion. Continue to check the stain before proceeding with rubbing until all traces are removed.

How to Reduce Fire-stain

• Apply flux liberally across all surfaces of the piece.

• There are pastes available that, when coated onto silver, can prevent fire-stain during annealing and soldering.

• Do not overheat the metal.

• Avoid the use of a small intense flame and maintain a neutral flame or reducing flame.

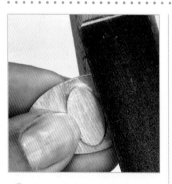

Once files have been used, the file marks also have to be removed. To do so will require a less abrasive material, such as emery papers or sticks. Using emery sticks allows greater and more even pressure to be applied.

Small pieces of wrapped emery paper can be used to get into spaces close to joins and seams.

Tips

• When working to remove fire-stain, continue to check the piece against a white background to prevent over-filing an area.

• Ensure each grade of sanding is carried out in a different direction, so the previous scratches and marks are easy to distinguish and then remove.

Polishing and Finishing

Polishing and finishing removes light scratches and marks caused during manufacture and soldering. These stages must only take place after all fire-stain and deep scratches have been taken care of.

Finding a Finish

To understand how to polish and finish you will need to know the various finishes that can be achieved:
• High polish mirror finish—shiny and highly reflective
• Satin finish—matte with a soft look
• Brushed finish—matte but with more texture and perhaps grains produced from the equipment used, be it wire brushes or abrasive papers

Whatever finish you wish to achieve, it is always important to clean the piece properly first. Be aware that dark gray shadows caused by fire-stain and deep scratches can still be quite visible on matte or brushed surfaces, which often highlight the imperfections more. There are many types of equipment and materials for polishing and finishing, many applied using a polishing motor, be it a hand-held flexible shaft or a secured motorized mop system.

Polishing Motors

To polish a piece against a polishing motorized mop or a pendant motor mop, safety procedures must be followed at all times:
• Practice and test on scrap pieces of metal first of all, so that you become familiar with the functions and workings of the equipment.
• Loose clothing must not be worn and hair should be tied back securely. Avoid wearing any pieces of jewelry on your hands or wrist.
• Protective eyewear should be worn to stop any stray parts or uncontrolled jewelry from hitting the eye area.
• Concentration and control are required, so do not speak or be distracted by others while using this machine—this poses danger to the piece and yourself.
• In case an accident does occur, always know how to turn the machine off quickly.
• Ensure the polishing motor has a ventilation system that removes the air containing polishing particles, or, if using a hand-held system, wear a face mask.

Polishing Lathe

There are various mops to choose from. You can select soft cotton mops for a mirror finish or, for a satin frosted finish, a bristle mop can be used instead. In addition, a polishing motor can house ring mops that can polish the inside of a ring shank. If you consider the mop as a clock face with the top as 12 o'clock, your pieces should always be held against the mop between 4 and 5 o'clock. If you position your piece too high, the speed of the motor can drag it away from you. Before switching on the polishing motor, your piece must be held securely and comfortably. Consider the areas you wish to polish and how you will hold the piece, remembering the strength of the motor at all times. Certain areas can be masked with masking tape to create multi-surface finishes to your piece. Apply polishing compound to the mop when it is spinning and held against the mop at around the 4 and 5 o'clock position. Once the mop is coated, begin polishing. Throughout the polishing process, repeat coating the mop with compound when necessary.

To polish the internal shank of a ring, a mounted felt cone can be applied to the motor. The same rules of polishing should be practiced and a firm grip of the ring must be ensured before placing onto the mop. Never place the ring up to a tapered part where it is a tight fit, as the ring will be pulled off the jeweler hand too easily. When polishing, always keep to the end as close as possible.

Hand-Held Flexible Shaft System or Pendant Motor

For a jeweler who does not have access to a polishing motor, a hand-held pendant motor is sufficient. This is an extremely useful piece of equipment that can house a variety of jewelry tools, from drills to small polishing mops. There are many shapes and types of mops, ranging from soft for a high polish finish through to the brass wire types that can be used to achieve a polish finish on a textured or patterned surface. The benefits of using a mop on a hand-held pendant motor is being able to reach small and awkward areas, but care should be taken not to allow the mop to be applied consistently in one area as grooves or uneven polish marks could occur.

When working with mechanical equipment, be it a hand-held flexible shaft or a polishing lathe, you must hold the piece securely and steadily. With a hand-held flexible shaft, the best place to hold the piece is on the bench peg; on a polishing lathe, you hold the piece against the lathe itself.

To apply polishing compound onto the hand-held mop, place the block of compound onto the workbench and hold securely with one hand. Start the mop and, as it rotates, bring it to touch lightly against the polish.

Once the mop is coated in the compound, stop the motor. Repeat this process as and when required during polishing.

While polishing a flat surface, continue to keep the mop moving. Holding it still will cause an uneven removal of metal and an irregularly polished surface.

Chain should be wrapped securely around a support, such as a wooden block or stick, before the mop—or polishing lathe—is applied.

Pieces can be covered with masking tape before polishing in order to add interest and variation to the finish.

Polish the piece as usual. The covered areas will remain matte, while other sections are polished.

Polishing Compounds

All polishing mops, be they hand-held or secured polishing lathes, must be used with polishing compounds. Start the process on a hard or medium mop with an abrasive such as Tripoli or carborax, both of which are available in bar form and, when applied to the mop, can remove fine scratches and light fire-stain.

Once an abrasive compound has been used, the piece should be cleaned in warm soapy water prior to being polished on a softer mop with a polishing compound such as rouge or dialux. Again, once the polishing is completed, ensure all traces of polishing compound are removed with a soft brush and soapy water. Always use just one type of polishing compound on any mop and wash the pieces between uses of different types to prevent contamination.

Tumble or Barrel Polisher

These polishers consist of a barrel containing metal ball bearings or rough stone pieces. When a piece of jewelry is placed inside, the barrel rotates, polishing or matting the piece, depending on the material used inside the drum. This is a time-saving and low-maintenance piece of equipment for polishing products such as chain or cast items. These can be thrown into the polisher and left until the desired finish is achieved. However, this type of polisher is not practical for all pieces of jewelry and can cause pieces to become distorted or damaged.

Hand Polishing

Hand polishing was the option prior to the invention of all these motorized tools. But there are still instances when a jeweler chooses to hand polish their piece, perhaps because of the type of finish they wish to achieve, or perhaps because the piece is too delicate or awkwardly shaped to be applied to a motorized system.

Suede-covered sticks and suede cloths Round, flat, or half-round sticks are glued with pieces of suede before being coated with polishing compound. The stick is then rubbed against the metal until a polish finish is achieved. To remove any fine scratches, first apply abrasive compounds such as Tripoli or carborax to one stick or cloth, then use a separate cloth or stick with a polishing compound such as rouge or dialux for the final polish. Surprisingly, a high-standard polished finish can be achieved with this process, in particular with the use of rouge powder and a suede cloth.

Thrumming threads This type of tool is for use on pierced-out areas, holes, and difficult-to-access spots. The thread is secured at one end. Polish is applied to it, then jewelry is threaded through and moved up and down, polishing the surface. As with any polishing, start with an abrasive compound and then change threads and apply a polish.

Emery papers and sticks These are used for the removal of fire-stain, marks, and scratches, but can also create a matte finish. Depending on the grade of paper used, you can achieve either a fine satin finish or a coarser rough finish. The paper can be used by hand or wrapped around a split mandrel that is inserted in a hand-held flexible shaft. Emery paper is positioned in the slot and wrapped around the pin before being used like a mop. This technique can be used for cleaning as well as polishing.

Wire and bristle brushes A selection of these made from different materials can offer a surface finish to a piece. They can be used by brushing in one direction or in circular movements to create a scratched matte finish.

Wire wool Similarly to wire brushes, a small piece of this can be sanded against a metal surface to create a matte finish. Household wire and plastic scourers can also be used to sand and create satin finishes on your metal. Test various types of scourers on scrap metals before you use them on your finished piece.

Liquid polish There are a number of these available from the store in liquid or wadding options. Once the piece has been finished with the finest of emery papers, a liquid polish is applied to give it a high polish. Although this method will not create the brilliant mirror finish of a motorized mop, it does offer a satisfactory result.
When working with liquid, use a soft household polishing cloth or a leather chamois. Wadding can be applied directly from the tin, moving the wadding against the metal in one direction. Once buffing is complete, remove traces of the polish with a clean, soft cloth.

Polishing cloths These are impregnated with polish and are available for silver or gold/platinum. By buffing the metal, you can remove tarnishes and fine marks. A cloth can be hand-held and rubbed against the metal, or fold the cloth and lay it on a flat surface; then place the piece of jewelry on top and rub vigorously against the cloth until a high shine has been achieved.

Plating and Coloring

Plating or coloring a metal can add another dimension to jewelry. It can also cover any marks, such as fire-stain; offer an anti-tarnish coating; or, with plating, give the illusion of a higher-value metal.

To cover the surface of a metal, the following options are most widely used.

Electroplating

Plating is used to cover the original metal to give the illusion of a higher value metal, or to cover marks such as fire-stain. The process involves coating one metal onto the surface of another by electric current. The metal is immersed in a solution of metal salt of the desired coating. A negative current is then applied to the metal. A good surface is required for plating. It has to be clean and mark-free.

Plating is normally carried out by an expert. Although the technique can be achieved within a small jewelry workshop, the plating chemicals are highly toxic. There are various types of colored plating available: yellow, rose, and white gold; gun metal; and rhodium plate. A plating expert will be able to offer advice on each and can plate your pieces at a reasonable cost. Plating workshops can be found in most cities.

The thickness of plating is determined and gauged by the micron: the higher the micron, the thicker the plating and ultimately the higher the cost. With a thinner coating, the durability is reduced. Obviously, a ring will be exposed to higher wear than, say, a pair of earrings, which may not necessarily need such a thick coat of plating.

Oxidizing Metal

When oxidizing metal, follow health and safety procedures by wearing latex gloves to protect your hands.

1 Pour a small amount of oxidizing solution into a plastic dish. Pre-mixed solution is used in the sequence detailed here.

2 Entire pieces can be immersed in the solution for 5–10 seconds. The oxidizing solution reacts quickly with silver and will produce a dark, intense black-blue color in very little time.

3 Once the 5–10-second period has passed and the surface color is achieved, remove the piece with plastic tweezers and wash in running water. Dry with a soft cloth.

Oxidization

This is the most commonly used coloring method for silver. As very few materials and equipment are used, it is a good choice for a jeweler. It gives a black finish to the metal by using a liver of sulfur solution. This solution can be created by dissolving potassium sulfide in warm water, but pre-mixed solutions are available from jewelry suppliers. Either immerse the entire piece in the solution for even coverage, or apply to the desired areas using a clean brush. An entirely immersed piece can have areas polished off to create a contrasting finish of black against a highly polished or matte silver.

Enameling

Enamels are glass-type substances that can be applied to metal, and heated until they melt and fuse together. The enamels available are opaque, translucent, bright/vibrant, or in soft pastel colors, while the finishes can be glossy or matte. Enamel is available in powder or nugget form. Enameling can only be done on gold, silver, and copper.

To melt/fire enamel, the piece is normally placed in a heated kiln until the enamel fuses, but blow torches can also be used. Whichever method you choose, make sure the solder you use around the enamel area has a high enough melting temperature to survive the firing process. See "Solders and Fluxes" on pages 34–37.

Resin or Cold Enamels

Resin enamels are an alternative to glass enamels and do not require heat. They are essentially a colored plastic that is applied to the jewelry piece and allowed to cure and adhere. Resin enamels are available in both translucent and opaque options. They should only be applied during the final stages, when all soldering work has been completed, as any heat or chemicals would damage them.

GOLD PLATED NECKLACE
KATIE LEES

Plating this silver piece in gold gives it both a richness of color and increases its perceived value. Prior to applying any type of color or coating to a piece, the finish should be immaculate. The common misconception that a coating will hide any imperfections is false and any blemishes, be they excess solder or file marks, will be emphasized when colored.

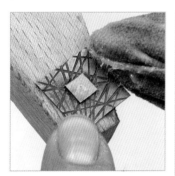

4 Coat the piece with beeswax using a soft cloth. This gives the oxidized color a protective layer which will prolong it.

5 Polishing an oxidized piece that has engraved areas will create a polished part with oxidized engraved detailing, which can add textural depth.

6 To color specific areas, apply the oxidizing solution with a fine brush.

7 Certain areas can be protected with masking tape before using a brush to apply the solution. Once the area is coated, wash the piece and then remove the masking tape. The black color works well against the whiteness of the silver.

Chapter 4
Projects

This chapter offers individual projects for you to carry out, beginning with some simple but beautiful jewelry pieces and progressing to more complex articles with multiple solder joins. You will be led through every soldering stage of the projects, allowing you to produce and finish each piece of jewelry or accessory on your own. Each step of the construction process is fully illustrated, alongside a list of the tools and materials required. An unassembled view of the jewelry piece offers an easy-to-understand visual for solder placement.

As you move through this chapter, you will carry out the techniques that have been explained in the previous chapter, gaining extensive experience of essential soldering techniques across a broad spectrum of metals, applications, and common jewelry pieces. With this experience, you can then turn to producing your own stunning designs and styles.

ESSENTIAL TOOLS
For every project you will need:

- Shears for cutting solder paillons
- Borax dish to hold snippets of solder
- Stainless steel tweezers for placing solder paillons
- Revolving turntable, though not essential, is always useful for accessing all angles of your piece
- Firebrick or other suitable surface for soldering on
- Torch
- Dish of cool water for quenching
- Pickle solution and brass tweezers. Stainless steel tweezers should not be used with pickle solution as the steel contaminates the pickle.
- Selection of needle files and various grades of emery paper. Specific grades or files may be mentioned in individual tools lists.
- Selection of polishing mops.

Please note the metal and measurements listed in these projects are just a suggestion and adjustments should be made according to your own size or preference. Where extra metal is required to allow the piece to be held, this is mentioned in specific projects. However, do consider for each project that you may need to use extra metal to allow an edge for solder to flow so you might need to increase the dimensions marginally.

Textured Ring

This project will guide you through the steps of applying surface decoration, shaping and forming a ring shank, preparing a join for solder, and the soldering process.

TOOLS AND EQUIPMENT

* Metal ruler
* Metal dividers
* Selection of needle files
* Piercing saw
* Emery paper
* Borax cone, dish, and brush
* Hard silver solder
* Powder rouge, water, container, and brush
* Rawhide mallet
* Ring mandrel
* Half round nosed pliers
* Round emery stick

SKILL LEVEL 💍

TECHNIQUES USED

* Sweat soldering
* Soldering on textured surfaces
* Using solder inhibitors

When making a ring, the first consideration is the ring size and width. The wider the ring, the more you have to allow a little extra in size to allow the ring to fit well. For example, if you have a ring made from ¹⁄₁₆ in (1mm) wire, size 5¼, a wider band of ³⁄₁₆ in (5mm) may require the ring to be half a size larger. The wider a ring is, the more of your finger it makes contact with and the tighter it will feel. Try on ring sizers of various widths to see the difference—try on two rings of the same size, one with a narrow band and one with a wide band. Despite being technically the same size, the wider band will fit more tightly.

To make a ring solder well, the ends must meet flush, with the top and bottom edges lining up exactly with each other. Rings made from thinner sheet are much easier to match up—if thick wire is used, you will need to take extra care to make the ends butt well. Any gaps will be difficult to

solder and will leave a very visible channel and solder seam. When making the ends of a ring meet, do not worry about keeping the round shape of the ring, as once it has been successfully soldered it can be re-shaped.

Solder should always be applied to the inside shank of a ring so it remains as hidden as possible. If you are applying additional pieces to the surface, try to carry out as much of this work as possible while the shank is flat, prior to shaping and soldering the ring. Obviously there will be parts that can only be applied once the ring has been shaped and soldered.

In this project, you will also use a solder inhibitor. Solder inhibitors can prove crucial in difficult soldering tasks, as they prevent previously soldered joins from flowing and also prevent the flow of solder onto unwanted areas, such as the textured and patterned areas of this ring.

MATERIALS:

Central piece
½ x ½ x ¹⁄₃₂ in (12 x 12 x 0.8mm) silver sheet

Ring shank
2½ x ⅜ x ¹⁄₁₆ in
(65 x 10 x 1.3mm) silver sheet

HOW TO WORK OUT THE METAL LENGTH FOR A RING

To calculate the length of metal required for a ring, measure the finger with a ring sizer and convert to inches in length. Or if you know the diameter of the shank you wish to make, add the metal thickness and multiply by 3.142.

½ in (12mm)

½ in (12mm)

⅜ in (10mm)

2½ in (65mm)

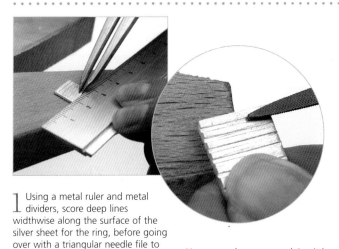

1 Using a metal ruler and metal dividers, score deep lines widthwise along the surface of the silver sheet for the ring, before going over with a triangular needle file to enhance the depth. This sample has been created by using a mechanical engraving tool, which creates equally spaced lines.

However, when you are doing it by hand, do not worry about irregularities, which will add to the unique appearance of the ring.

2 Pierce the central ring shape, then file and neaten the edges before checking that it fits flush against the textured sheet. Do not worry if it sits off the shank edges slightly as this can be filed later.

3 Rub the pierced shape with emery paper, turn it upside down on a firebrick, and paint with flux. Use tweezers to place hard silver solder snippets close to the edge. Heat with a small to medium flame and allow solder to melt and flow along the surface.

4 Once the piece has been cleaned in pickle solution and water, use a coarse emery paper to remove any excess solder or bumps. Wash and dry, and then paint with flux.

5 Coat the central part of the textured piece with flux and then place the pierced shape carefully, solder side down, onto the central part of the textured piece. Using a mixture of powder rouge and water, paint the area to either side of the fluxed area. A gap between the flux and the rouge must be left so the two do not mix together: Doing so may prevent solder from flowing in the necessary direction.

6 Adjust the torch to a medium-sized neutral flame and heat the base piece. As there are some gaps behind the pierced piece, the change of color to a dull red will be visible. During this color change, circle the flame onto the smaller piece and solder will flow as both pieces become dull red in color. Remove the heat.

7 Once the piece has been allowed to cool, quench in water and place in pickle solution. After drying the piece off, hammer and shape around a ring mandrel. Make the ends meet by tapping down with a rawhide mallet and using half round nose pliers.

8 Apply a layer of flux on the ring, paying attention to the seam but avoiding the previous solder join—this should prevent the solder from flowing into the texture. Place solder on the seam inside the ring, which will also prevent solder from flooding the outer surface texture and ensure any excess solder remains inside.

9 Using the top of the flame, heat gently around the ring to dry the flux and adhere the solder to the piece. Then take the heat to the opposite side of the ring from the seam so the metal will start to expand and push the seam tight together.

10 Circle the flame over the entire ring. Once an even heat has been achieved, focus the flame around the seam area. The silver should start to change to dark red, before solder begins to flow. As the solder runs, direct the flow down the channel until it has run evenly, then remove the heat.

11 Allow the soldered piece to cool for at least one minute, until no longer glowing, before quenching in water. It is important to remove all traces of the rouge or any applied solder inhibitors before placing the piece into pickle solution, which will prevent contamination of the solution. To remove the rouge, use a soft brush and soap under running water.

12 Re-shape the ring on a ring mandrel and remove any excess solder with small round files and a round emery stick, taking care not to take away too much metal from the inside of the shank, which would change the size and shape of the ring.

FERN RING
CHARLIE HIGH

The main body of this piece has been textured and pierced prior to the central wire piece being sweat soldered. Once the two parts were successfully soldered together, it was formed into the ring shape. The oxidized finish on the texture and the highly polished wire marry well together to form a beautiful piece.

Bezel-Setting Ring

One of the most commonly used settings is the rub-over or bezel. It is simple to make, although if you are soldering onto the top level of a curved ring shank, care must be taken to align the setting with the shape of the ring before soldering.

TOOLS AND EQUIPMENT

* Ring mandrel
* Round nosed pliers
* Piercing saw and fine saw blade
* Borax cone, dish, and brush
* Reverse-action tweezers
* Hard and medium silver solder
* Rawhide mallet
* Half round ring pliers
* Dividers
* Scribe or needle file
* Selection of round and half round files
* Emery paper (various grades)
* Round and half round emery sticks (various grades)

SKILL LEVEL 👑 👑

TECHNIQUES USED

* Butt soldering

B ezel, or rub-over settings, are often used for cabochon, rather than faceted cut stones, as they tend to allow less light to travel through the stone. However, some rub-over settings are opened at the sides or back to allow light to enter. The benefits of using a rub-over setting are security of stone and the variety of shapes that can be made.

When creating and soldering a setting, consider the height you wish to make it. The wall of the setting has to be high enough to house the stone securely, but not so high that it covers too much of the stone. The optimum height of the setting wall is just covering the beginning of the curve of the stone. Each stone is individual—even if they have the same diameter or karat weight, the height may vary greatly for each. When

making a setting, ensure you measure against the exact stone you are working with.

Although simple, this rub-over setting has to be aligned with a curved base prior to soldering, and any error in alignment will be quite noticeable. Therefore, it is best practice to spend as much time as possible filing and fitting the setting to the ring prior to soldering.

To allow the setting to sit on the curved base and also have a flat base on which the stone can rest, this setting has a flat bezel within. A bezel can be used within a rub-over setting when the setting is going to be applied onto a curved base (like this ring), for a setting with an open back to allow light to pass through, or when the design of the setting is too high for the height of the stone and a seat is required to house it.

MATERIALS:

Ring shank
2½ x ¼ in (60 x 8mm)
D-section silver wire

Rub-over setting
1 x ½ x ¹⁄₃₂ in (24 x 8 x 0.8mm) silver sheet

Internal collet
¾ x ¹⁄₃₂ in (18 x 1mm) round silver wire

Stone
¼ in (7mm) diameter round cabochon stone

2½ in (60mm)

⅝ in (17mm)

1 in (24mm)

¼ in (8mm)

¾ in (18mm)

¼ in (6mm)

¼ in (7mm)

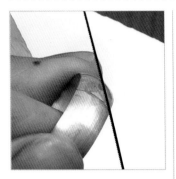

1 After annealing the D-shaped wire, form around a ring mandrel and use round nosed pliers to make the ends meet. To achieve the tightest fit for soldering, saw down the seam with a piercing saw and fine saw blade.

2 On a firebrick, paint the ring with flux and use tweezers to place a small paillon of hard silver solder on the top and the base, inside the shank along the seam. Applying the solder inside the seam allows any marks or solder stains to be filed away without damaging or changing the D-shaped curve of the outside of the ring.

3 With a medium-sized neutral flame, heat the ring from the opposite side to the seam to allow the piece to expand and close the seam more tightly. Circle the heat over the entire piece before heating around the seam area. Remove the heat when solder runs down the seam.

4 Once the ring has been cooled, quenched, and placed in pickle solution, wash with water. Dry off the ring and place onto a ring mandrel. Re-shape the ring with the help of a rawhide mallet.

5 Taking the length of silver sheet, anneal, shape, and join the ends with round nosed pliers. Check that the stone fits well by dropping it into the setting prior to soldering.

6 Flux the setting and apply hard silver solder to the top of the join or on the outside, as this will stop the solder from running internally, which would prevent the stone's insertion.

7 Again, as with the ring shank, using a medium-sized neutral flame, heat from the opposite side from the join to allow the metal to expand and push the ends tighter together, before applying the heat around the entire setting. Once the setting starts to heat and turn dark red, focus the heat around the join.

8 Allow the piece to cool, immerse it in pickle solution, and wash it. Re-shape the setting with half round ring pliers by inserting the curved arm inside the bezel and applying even pressure around the circumference.

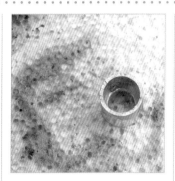

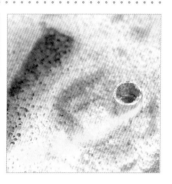

9 Using dividers, mark approximately 1/16 in (2mm) down into the bezel (this measurement is determined by the height of your stone: please refer to a stone setting book). This mark will be a guideline for positioning the internal collet for soldering.

10 Form an internal collet with your round wire. Make this as tight a fit within the setting as possible and then paint with flux. Also apply flux to the inside of the setting and its solder seam before forcing the collet into the marked position with a scribe or needle file.

11 Turn the setting upside down on a firebrick and apply hard solder on the seam between the inside of the bezel and the internal collet. Placing solder underneath the seat will prevent excess solder from running and disturbing the stone's platform.

12 With a medium-sized neutral flame, heat gently from the outside, on the opposite side from the join, and then the entire piece, inside and out. Once the pieces start to become hot, focus the heat on the inside, circling the inner collet and the area around it. As solder runs, remove the heat, cool, quench in water, and pickle.

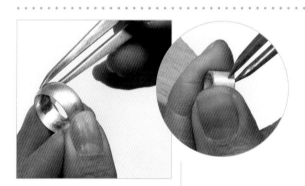

13 Using dividers, measure the height of the ring depth and mark this measurement on the setting. Using a saw and files, remove the excess metal between the ring and the setting, until the two join and fit well together.

Tip

Solder must be kept to the minimum, as any excess will cause the setting to become too tight, or the stone may sit up higher than intended and the setting will become too low to rub-over the stone.

14 Flux the setting, turn it upside down on a firebrick, and place the fluxed ring shank on top with the solder seam on the palm-side of the ring. This prevents heat re-opening the ring shank join and also allows for any future resizing of the ring. If required, steady and stabilize the ring with reverse-action tweezers. Heat the piece slightly and then apply fluxed medium silver solder. This will adhere to the awkward position of the seam.

15 Heat the ring shank first with a medium-sized neutral flame, then circle around the setting and the top of the shank. Once solder runs smoothly around the setting, remove heat, quench in cool water, and place in pickle. Clean the ring with files, emery paper, and emery sticks. If necessary, reduce the height of the setting by filing to fit to the height of the stone. Once the ring is polished, set the stone (refer to another book on rub-over or bezel setting) before applying a final polish.

Domed Earrings

This project leads you through the processes of pre-construction planning, sweat soldering, and forming. In addition, you will learn how to solder smaller or finer forms to a larger surface area.

TOOLS AND EQUIPMENT

* Tracing paper and pencil
* White gouache paint and clean paintbrush
* Scribe
* Piercing saw and saw blades
* Selection of needle files
* Reverse-action tweezers
* Borax cone, dish, and brush
* Hard and medium silver solders
* Doming block and punches
* Hand drill and ¹⁄₃₂ in (0.9mm) drill bit
* Selection of emery papers
* Selection of polishing mops for flexible shaft

SKILL LEVEL ⚭⚭

TECHNIQUES USED

* Sweat soldering
* Soldering of wire

Knowing when to solder is just as important as knowing how to solder. The construction of this pair of earrings is a fine example of where good planning is essential: If the soldering were carried out after forming, the project would be extremely difficult to carry out successfully. Understanding this teaches the value of setting plans in place, not only for the number of solder joins but for the stages too.

Tip
During production of "double" jewelry, such as earrings or cufflinks, make sure the matching pair are a mirror image of each other. The parts you fabricate should always be mirrored and not the same.

MATERIALS:

Silver sheet of ¹⁄₃₂ in (0.6mm) thickness to produce:
* 2 x ¾ in (18.5mm) diameter discs
* 2 x ⅜ in (10mm) diameter discs
* 2 x pierced shapes with widest points ⅝ x ¾ in (15.5 x 21mm)

2 earring post wires of ¹⁄₃₂ x ½ in (0.8 x 12mm) each

2 silver round belcher chains, approximately ¹⁄₁₆ in (2mm) round and 1¼ in (30mm) long

2 purchased silver earring backs (not shown)

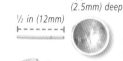

⅝ x ¾ in (15.5 x 21mm)

Approx. ⅛ in (4mm) deep

½ in (12mm)

¾ in (18.5mm)

Approx. ⅛ in (2.5mm) deep

⅜ in (10mm)

1¼ in (30mm)

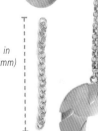

This earring project is also a good opportunity to practice the skills of sweat soldering, soldering of chain, and soldering of earring pins. The basics of soldering chain and findings are fundamental techniques used in many jewelry designs and constructions. Learning to make jump rings and chain is one of the first skills any jeweler will be taught (see pages 56–57). Chain is used in countless jewelry pieces, be it to suspend a finished necklace, to create a bracelet, or to join parts that require a fluid movement.

1 Using a pencil, draw the design onto tracing paper and then turn the page over and retrace the design. Place the tracing the right way up over a white-painted flat sheet of silver and draw over the outline. This will leave an imprint of the design on the white paint.

2 Using the design imprint, etch over the drawing with a scribe. When the mark is visible, remove the paint by washing in water.

3 Cut the shape carefully with a piercing saw, keeping the saw blade on the outside of the scribe mark. This will prevent you cutting into the shape and removing excess metal.

Soldering Small Pieces to a Larger Surface

- When soldering a small piece to a larger surface, always heat the large piece first and then bring the heat to the smaller piece to avoid melting the smaller component.

- Scribe lightly on the large piece where you want to place and solder the smaller piece, so that when both have been fluxed and heated you are able to see the exact position the piece should be applied to.

4 File until neat and even edges have been achieved, using a selection of fine needle files. Half-round, round, and triangular are all ideally shaped files for fitting into these areas.

5 To make a matching mirror pair of earrings, use the original pierced and filed shape but turned upside down. Place it on top of the silver sheet and draw around the shape with a scribe. Pierce with the saw, and file and neaten the edges, making sure it is a completely matching mirrored copy of the original shape.

6 Paint flux on the back of both pierced shapes and apply paillons of hard solder dotted close to the center. Normally, during sweat soldering, the snippets of solder are placed close to the edges to allow the flow to reach the borderlines. However, as the back of this piece is not completely covered, the snippets are kept away from the edges to avoid visible solder.

7 With both pieces positioned on a firebrick, switch the torch on to a medium-sized neutral flame. Heat with the torch held slightly away from the piece until the flux starts to dry, then bring the flame closer. Circle the pieces with flame until the solder flows. Once solder has run, cool for at least one minute, quench, and pickle.

8 Clean and sand down the solder with coarse emery paper to remove any lumps or bumps.

9 When the two pierced pieces fit flat against the two larger flat discs, flux one pierced piece and the large disc and position on a firebrick. Heat both with a medium-sized soft and neutral flame, watch the flux turn glassy, and then continue to move the torch. Once the solder seam appears to flow completely, remove the heat. Repeat the process for the matching earring.

10 Once the pieces have been allowed to cool, pickle and clean. Dry off, take to the doming block, and dome inward. Anneal and dome the two smaller discs.

11 Sand the two smaller domes in a figure eight on coarse emery paper. This will create a clean, flat top edge, in preparation for finishing at a later stage.

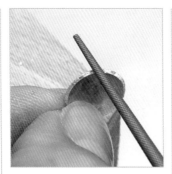

12 Taking your pre-bought chain and one of the smaller domes, file a very slight groove onto the top edge of the dome, where the jump ring will meet. Repeat the process for the second small dome.

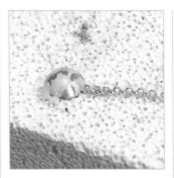

13 Flux the small dome, place upside down on a firebrick, and lay the chain beside the piece. Coat the last link of the chain with flux and slot into place against the pre-filed groove. Position the chain so the next link does not touch the solder area and do not flux the rest of the chain.

14 Heat the dome slightly until the flux has dried. Then, apply a tiny piece of fluxed solder to the seam between the two. The solder will stick in place. Heat the dome until it is a dull red color before carefully and quickly flicking the flame over the jump ring. The jump ring and chain will become heated very quickly, allowing solder to flow. Remove heat immediately after the flow of solder to prevent the chain from melting. Repeat for the second earring. Cool and pickle both.

15 File a groove in the two larger domes and fit the chain. Paint the end link of chain with flux and make that sure that the entire large dome is painted with flux to allow previous solder to flow.

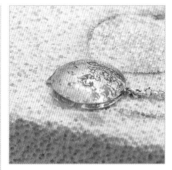

16 Direct a medium-sized neutral flame onto the dome first, as this is the larger of the two pieces. As the dome begins to change to a dull red color, allow the flame to flick over the jump ring. Solder will flow immediately. As soon as solder flows, remove the heat to prevent the chain from melting. Cool and pickle. Repeat for the second of the earrings.

17 Drill a slight indentation onto the top of the center of both small domes. Cut away just enough to allow the earring posts to be stabilized. Taking one of your pre-cut earring post wires, file a flat edge, paint with flux, and insert into the hole. Paint flux onto the dome and secure the earring post with reverse-action tweezers.

18 Place a paillon of medium solder so that it is touching the wire and the dome. Heat with a small neutral flame, making sure to heat the dome first. As it changes to a dull red color, bring the flame to the earring post to allow the solder to draw up. Remove the heat immediately after the solder flows. Allow the piece to cool before quenching and pickling.

19 Clean any excess solder or marks on the back of the earrings with emery paper. Continue to clean both earrings to pre-polished standard.

20 Polishing can be carried out with small polishing mops attached to a hand drill or flexible shaft. Pay close attention to the earring post to remove any sharp edges so it becomes safe and comfortable when threaded through pierced ears.

21 The final stage is to scratch finish the back surface of the larger domes. To do so, hold the dome against the bench-peg and, with a sharp scribe, score irregular marks. This will create a good contrast between the polished pierced shape and the backing dome.

Once the earrings are finished, silver earring backs can be threaded onto each post. A selection are readily available from jewelry suppliers.

Interchangeable Earrings

These simple silver wire drop earrings are enhanced by a gold heart detail. The earring design—and heart shape—are easily adapted in order to personalize your work.

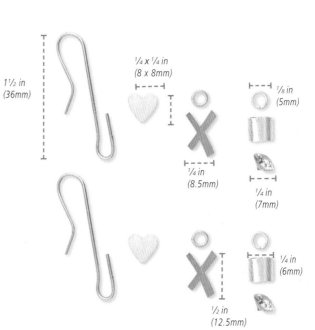

TOOLS AND EQUIPMENT

* Liquid flux and clean brush
* Small glass dish
* Hard silver solder
* Stainless steel tweezers
* Ring mandrel
* Round nosed pliers
* Bezel block
* Rawhide mallet
* Selection of needle files
* Reverse-action tweezers
* Borax cone, dish, and brush
* Various grades of emery paper
* Selection of polishing mops

SKILL LEVEL 💍💍

TECHNIQUES USED

* Soldering gold and silver together
* Soldering wire
* Soldering jump rings

Mixing different colored metals creates a strong visual impact on a piece of jewelry. In addition, adding a more expensive colored metal, even a small amount, also increases its value instantly. Adding a little gold to increase the retail value of a piece of silver jewelry is a tactic often employed by professional jewelers.

When soldering a combination of metals it is safer to follow the soldering techniques for the lowest-melting-temperature metal, as this will ensure that the metal does not melt. Therefore, when applying gold to silver, it is best to use silver soldering techniques. Silver solder should also be used as it has a lower melting point than gold and gold solders—and it is more cost-effective to use silver than gold. The soldering stages for this project are all quite simple, but care must be taken to solder the fine wire and metal without melting them. The silver wire is soldered prior to shaping, to make the soldering process easier.

MATERIALS:

Two gold hearts
¾ x ⅜ x ¹⁄₃₂ in (20 x 10 x 0.6mm)
9kt yellow gold sheet

Earring hoops
2 x 3 in (75mm) of ¹⁄₃₂ in
(0.9mm) round silver wire

Two crosses
⅜ x 1⅛ x ¹⁄₃₂ in (10 x 28 x
0.7mm) silver sheet
4 x ⅛ in- (5mm) outer-diameter
pre-made or bought round silver
jump rings

Set stone
2 bezel settings ¾ x ¼ x ¹⁄₃₂ in
(20 x 6 x 0.7mm)
2 x ¼ in (7mm) facetted stones

1½ in (36mm)

¼ x ¼ in (8 x 8mm)

⅛ in (5mm)

¼ in (8.5mm)

¼ in (7mm)

½ in (12.5mm)

¼ in (6mm)

Tips

- Always consider this question before you solder: Will the piece be easier to hold and fit closer for solder if it is shaped after soldering? Decide how you can make the soldering process easier.
- Liquid flux can assist in the soldering of fine parts that are at risk of moving during application or when heat expansion occurs with the use of borax flux. Liquid flux is easy to use and apply; it reduces the risk of parts moving, and requires no preparation.

EARRINGS

1 Place some liquid flux into a small glass dish and, using a clean brush on a firebrick, apply a coating onto the back of the gold heart and along the top of the silver wire. Due to the delicate nature of the heart and the wire, using the liquid flux will prevent expansion and movement of the two pieces when they are heated.

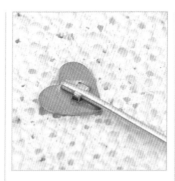

2 Cut two small snippets of hard silver solder and immerse them in the liquid flux, using stainless steel tweezers. Place one paillon of solder on either side of the wire, allowing the pieces to be in contact with both the silver wire and the gold heart.

3 As the pieces and the area for solder are quite small, heat the heart gently with a small neutral flame. Using a large flame will heat the area too quickly and blast the parts away.

4 Move the flame around the heart and then focus on the wire. The two pieces will become heated very quickly, so watch out for the solder running. As soon as the solder flows down the seam on both sides, withdraw the flame and allow the piece to cool for at least one minute, until the metal stops glowing, before quenching in water, then in pickle solution.

5 Clean any excess solder, then shape the earring wire by hand against the ring mandrel using round nosed pliers. This will also work-harden the earring wire, which will have annealed and softened during the heating process.

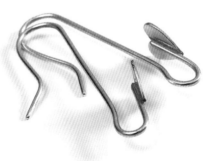

Once the earrings have been cleaned and polished at this stage, they are ready to be worn. Alternatively, they can be adorned with a choice of suspended drops—the production of which is demonstrated on the next pages.

STONE SET DROP

6 Construct a straight-sided bezel setting as illustrated in the "Bezel-Setting Ring" project on pages 97–99, but do not add an internal bezel. Taking the annealed bezel, insert it into a bezel block and hammer the punch with a rawhide mallet.

7 Once the straight bezel has been stretched and tapered in the bezel block, remove it. Using a round needle file, remove a small area of metal from the setting on which to position and fit a jump ring. Make sure the jump ring fits flush to the bezel.

Tip

It is advisable to position the bale onto the same place as the original solder seam on this setting. Doing so results in only one solder join, keeping the piece tidy with fewer areas to clean. During the planning stage of any piece, consider if additional parts can be soldered to previous joins. On a ring shank, it is best to work opposite the original seam to prevent the original seam from opening if multiple parts are being soldered and to allow an area for the ring to be cut and resized in the future if necessary.

8 Paint borax flux onto the surface of the bezel and place it with its larger-diameter end on the firebrick, as this will offer the most steady position. Heat it with a small neutral flame quickly and gently, then remove the flame. Place a pre-fluxed piece of hard silver solder onto the grooved area where the jump ring will be joined. The solder will immediately adhere and stay in position.

9 Paint flux onto the jump ring and hold it close to the join area with reverse-action tweezers. Using a small neutral flame, heat the bezel, circling around the entire piece and then focusing on the solder area. As the solder flows, bring the jump ring to touch the bezel and release the reverse-action tweezers before removing the heat. The jump ring will now be soldered.

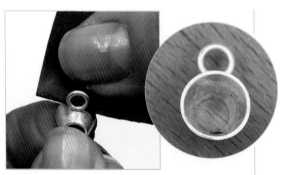

10 Once the piece has cooled until it is no longer glowing, quench it and place in pickle solution. Wash and clean any excess solder or marks with emery paper before polishing. Repeat stages 6–10 with the second stone setting. Once both are complete, rub-over-set the stone.

ARROW AND CROSSES DROP

11 Taking the pierced and engraved drops, fit the soldered jump rings into each piece, making sure there are no gaps and that they fit together well on both sides.

12 Flux with liquid flux and place flat onto the firebrick. Make sure the brick you are using has a clean and uniform flat surface so the pieces sit evenly. If the surface is uneven, the jump rings will be soldered at an unwanted angle.

13 Place one paillon of fluxed solder at each side of the jump ring, ensuring the solder touches both the jump ring and the cross. Repeat and place the second cross alongside the first cross. Make sure the second cross is the mirror image of the first.

16 Complete the pair of crosses by polishing on mops. Once polished, the pair can be suspended individually from the heart earrings or together with the stone set drops.

14 Heat one cross first with a medium-sized neutral flame, taking care to dry the flux and not to blow the solder off. Once the piece has reached an optimum heat and started to turn dull red, turn the focus of the flame on each drop. The solder will flow quickly, joining the jump ring and the cross. Repeat for the second cross.

15 When both drops have been soldered, leave until no longer glowing, quench, and pickle. Clean with small needle files if required, or work with just emery paper. Take care when cleaning not to over-emery areas, particularly the jump ring, as you can take away too much metal, causing the round shape of the jump ring to be distorted.

Wire-Detail Bracelet

This bracelet is fabricated from chain and square wire, formed to give it depth and structure. It costs a great deal less to produce than if it were constructed from solid sheet pieces.

TOOLS AND EQUIPMENT

* Hard and medium silver solder
* Ring mandrel
* Flat stake
* Rawhide mallet
* Round nosed pliers
* Half round nosed pliers
* Piercing saw and blades
* Borax cone, dish, and brush
* Round domed mandrel
* Reverse-action tweezers
* Flat ended pliers
* Selection of emery papers
* Selection of polishing mops

SKILL LEVEL 👂👂

TECHNIQUES USED

* Butt soldering
* Soldering jump rings
* Soldering wire
* Multiple solder joins

Wire can be shaped and formed into all kinds of intricate detailing, offering a light and delicate effect. But the great adaptability of wire means that it can also be developed into heavier-weight, chunky, and more structured pieces.

Due to the high number of solder joins in this piece, you will need to use solders with a variety of hardnesses. It is always safer to use hard solder for as many joins as possible before moving on to the next lower-melting-point solder.

It is often good practice to use homemade chain, and on many occasions the style you are looking for may be better suited to personally designed chain. However, for this project, as in many other circumstances, it is actually best to purchase ready-made chain. Making your own chain is time-consuming and costly, whereas countless types of chain can be purchased easily.

MATERIALS:

9½ in (240mm) of silver trace chain
39½ in (1m) of ¹⁄₃₂ in (1.2mm) square silver wire

NOTE:

This bracelet has been created in an average size of 7½ in (19cm). If you wish to decrease or increase, adjust the length of the chain used.

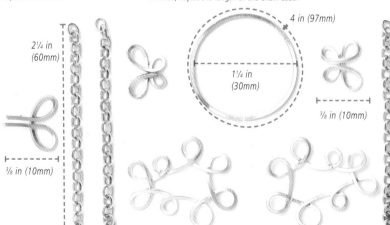

2¼ in (60mm)

⅜ in (10mm)

4 in (97mm)

1¼ in (30mm)

⅜ in (10mm)

⅜ in (10mm)

1¼ in (30mm)

Tip

Bear in mind when designing and creating pieces of jewelry such as rings, bangles, and bracelets that their structure should be strong enough to withstand bumps and bashes. In this project, the use of square section wire offers a stronger and more durable structure to the wire shapes of the bracelet.

1 Make a 1¼ in- (30mm) diameter ring with ¹⁄₃₂ in (1.2mm) square wire. To calculate the length of wire required, follow this equation: diameter x 3.142 + (thickness of wire x 2) = 4 in (97mm) (rounded off). Butt join the ends and solder with hard silver solder, following the same process as for soldering jump rings (see pages 56–57).

2 Once the soldered ring has been placed in pickle solution and cleaned, reshape it on a ring mandrel. When the ring is perfectly round, place on a flat stake and hit with a rawhide mallet to make it as flat as possible.

3 Using approximately 8¾ in (220mm) of the ¹⁄₃₂ in (1.2mm) square wire, twist and bend the shape with freehand and pliers. Do not worry about replicating the design shown here exactly.

4 Repeat step 3 to produce a second wire shape. Cut the ends off both shapes with a piercing saw to create a flat plane that will sit flush with the matching end of the other wire piece, ready for soldering. Do not use shears as this will pinch the end and cause an ill-fitting solder seam.

5 Using approximately 8¾ in (220mm) of square wire, make the two wire side shapes and the clasp and hook ends. To finish the hook clasps, use pliers to double the wire back onto itself.

6 Taking all the pre-fabricated wire parts, cut their ends with saw blades and fit to the opposite points. If required, manipulate the ends freehand or use pliers until all the ends fit well for soldering.

7 All parts are now ready for soldering. Place one of the main large wire components onto the firebrick. Paint with flux, heat very slightly with a medium-sized reducing flame to allow the parts to become hot, and then apply fluxed hard silver solder paillons onto each join.

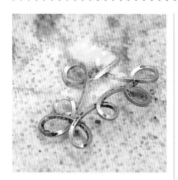

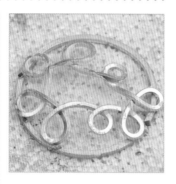

8 Heat with a neutral flame, taking care to move continuously to prevent any parts of the wire from melting. The wire will become hot very quickly so pay close attention to its color. Once the entire piece has been heated, concentrate around the seam area, moving the flame in circles. As soon as solder runs, withdraw heat and repeat with the next join. Once complete, allow the piece to become cool, then pickle and wash before repeating the process for the second shape.

9 Take one of the cleaned soldered wire pieces and place it onto a round domed mandrel. If you do not have access to this tool, you can adapt a household object such as a curved wooden bowl, round metal door handle, or even a children's round wooden toy. Using a rawhide mallet, tap gently to form the piece. Repeat with the second part.

10 Check the formed central parts fit well against the top and base of the ring. If required, manipulate with your hands or pliers until the solder points all touch securely.

11 Place onto a firebrick and apply small snippets of hard silver solder to all the joins where the two pieces meet. If you find the snippets do not stay secured, heat the parts gently and apply fluxed pieces of solder.

12 Heat with a medium-sized neutral flame. The wire will become hot quickly so take care to keep the flame moving and to remove it as soon as a join is flooded with solder. Once all the joins have been soldered, remove heat, allow to cool, then place in pickle solution.

13 Turn the piece upside down and flux the previous join before placing onto the firebrick. Place the second central wire part on top and position solder onto the seams before soldering. Allow the piece to cool before quenching and placing in pickle solution.

14 For the remaining side and clasp pieces, place each on the firebrick and paint with flux. Allow the flame to flicker over the pieces so they become hot enough for fluxed solder paillons to adhere.

15 Heat each component with a medium-sized neutral flame. They will become hot very quickly, allowing solder to flow almost instantly. Remove the heat as soon as solder has run to prevent melting.

16 After cleaning all the parts, take the side component and set it up with the circular part. Allow the piece to lean against the ring: If you have a problem balancing, use reverse-action tweezers to hold the parts in place. Place a snippet of hard silver solder on each side of the part, allowing it to touch both of the components.

17 Gently heat the join area with a medium-sized neutral flame. Avoid heating any other areas, but if any of the previous joins start to open (solder melt), then the solder should flow as the entire piece has been coated in flux. Repeat this process for the opposite side and then allow the piece to cool before cleaning.

18 Using the pre-bought lengths of chain, cut the last jump ring on the end of each. Link one chain up with the central component and close the link using two pairs of tapered end pliers. Round nosed and flat ended pliers have been used here. Repeat this process for the second chain.

19 Open the last links on the opposite ends of the two pieces of chain and link up with the clasp. Close the jump rings, making sure that the ends fit tightly together for soldering.

Tip

To allow sufficient wire for constructing pieces and extra at the ends for holding with pliers, it is always best to use a length of wire that is longer than required. Bear in mind that excess can be removed, but, if you work with too little, you may have to start again.

20 Place the piece on a firebrick and flux the opened links. Heat slightly and then apply wet fluxed medium silver solder. The solder has to be as small as possible as the join is tiny. Excess solder may flow into the other jump rings in the chain, soldering them together.

21 Heat the seam area of the jump ring with a small needle flame. Pay close attention as the link will heat at a very high speed and solder will run immediately. Any delay in removing heat will cause the jump ring to melt.

22 Repeat stages 19–21 on the other side of the bracelet. Once all of the components have been linked together and soldered successfully, any excess solder can be removed with emery paper and the piece can be polished with polishing mops.

Studded Bangle

Bangles offer an array of design opportunities to the jeweler, from their shape, mechanism, and construction to the decoration applied. Their relative size provides plenty of surface to decorate.

TOOLS AND EQUIPMENT

* Round bangle mandrel
* Rawhide mallet
* Liquid flux and clean brush
* Hard and medium silver solder
* Planishing hammer
* Paper, protractor, and compass
* Scribe
* Hand drill and 1/16 in (1.5mm) drill bit
* Doming block and punches
* Coarse emery paper
* Half round needle file
* T-pins
* Half D-section and half flat parallel pliers
* Large flat and "D-shaped" files
* Selection of emery papers and sticks
* Liver of sulfur or pre-mixed oxidizing solution

SKILL LEVEL ⚭

TECHNIQUES USED

* Multiple solder joins
* Soldering of wire

Bangles can be fabricated and formed into all shapes and sizes, be it round, square, oval, or even octagonal. They can also be open backed, closed, or hinged (see pages 128–131) and produced from an array of shapes and sizes of wires. As bangles tend to be larger in size than other types of jewelry, lengthy solder joins may be required. During the design process of larger jewelry pieces, consider their weight and how they will sit and feel on the wearer. Consider the amount of metal required and decide if this is appropriate, not only in terms of weight and comfort but also cost.

When preparing to solder a lengthy seam, ensure the pieces meet tightly together and, if necessary, secure them with binding wire. In this

project the outer rings have been made slightly small to ensure they fit tightly to the internal bangle. During soldering, remember to heat the pieces equally and to guide the solder along the seam with the flame (keeping in mind that solder always travels toward heat).

When you are making a bangle or any piece that requires forming or shaping, consider which components can be soldered prior to forming. It is much easier to solder onto a flat surface than an area that is formed or a curved plane. Of course, there are details that can be applied only once the bangle or piece has been formed and to do so may require some filing and fitting of the pieces to allow a flush fit and a larger area for soldering.

MATERIALS:

Center of bangle
8 x 3/8 x 1/32 in (200 x 10 x 1mm) silver sheet

Borders
2 x 8¼ in (205mm) of 1/16 in (2mm) square silver wire

Decoration
4 x ¼ in- (6mm) diameter disks of 1/32 in (0.8mm) thick silver sheet

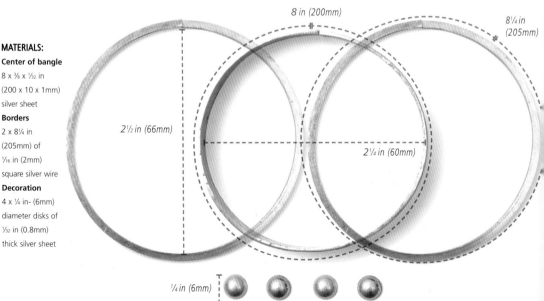

8 in (200mm)

8¼ in (205mm)

2½ in (66mm)

2¼ in (60mm)

¼ in (6mm)

1 Taking the length of silver sheet and the two wire pieces, anneal them. Form them around a bangle mandrel using a rawhide mallet. Manipulate with your hands to ensure the ends meet flush. Do not worry about keeping the perfect round shape of the bangles, as they can be reshaped after soldering.

2 Paint liquid flux onto the middle bangle section and place onto a firebrick. Position snippets of hard silver solder on the top of the seam.

3 Heat with a medium to large flame on the opposite side of the bangle from the seam at first, to allow expansion of the metal to push the ends closer together.

4 Continue to heat the bangle, moving the flame across the entire surface before concentrating on the seam and surrounding area. As the seam area starts to heat, the solder will run. When the flow of solder has moved down the seam evenly, remove the heat and allow the piece to cool until no longer glowing. Quench and pickle.

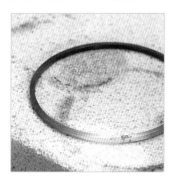

5 Repeat the soldering process, steps 2–4, on both outer bangle borders. Again, wait until both pieces are no longer glowing before quenching in water and placing in pickle solution. To get rid of the acidic pickle solution in the domes, place the piece in a solution of water and bicarbonate of soda, and boil for 5–10 minutes.

6 Remove all three bangles from the pickle solution, wash, and dry. Re-shape them on the bangle mandrel by hammering with a rawhide mallet. If the mandrel used is tapered, make sure the bangle sides are even by threading the bangle through from both sides and tapping with a rawhide mallet.

7 Fit the top and base borders to the wider central bangle. You will find that the two borders will be slightly too small to fit. To make them fit as tightly as possible, place the base edge bangle back onto a bangle mandrel and hammer gently with a planishing hammer to slightly stretch. Hammer all around, but only a few knocks before checking against the bangle. If you hammer too much there is a risk of the piece becoming too loose a fit.

8 Once the central and the bottom edge bangles fit tightly together, paint flux onto both and place on a firebrick. Make sure flux is on the outer and inner surfaces of both bangles, as these will meet for soldering. Place small paillons of solder along the top of the outer bangle, touching the inner bangle surface.

9 Heat the bangle pieces with a medium to large neutral flame. Start with the flame farther away to avoid blowing the paillons of solder off. Once the flux and solder pieces are dry and secure, bring the flame close and circle the entire piece. As both pieces start to change to dull red, solder will begin to flow. Use the flame to direct the solder flow around the circumference of the join—a revolving turntable can help.

10 Once the piece has been allowed to cool, quench and place in pickle solution. Wash and dry off before fitting the second border section. Place the piece onto a firebrick with the soldered border facing the top. Paint with flux and place solder snippets onto the top of the border bangle. Make sure the solder touches both the inner bangle and outer border bangle.

11 Turn the torch to a medium to large neutral flame and circle heat around the parts. Use a turntable to rotate the piece to allow even heat distribution. As the piece starts to heat and change to dull red in color, concentrate the flame on the seam area, again using the rotating action to view the entire seam and all angles.

12 Once the soldered bangle has been cleaned, use a protractor and compass to draw a circle and mark four 90-degree angles in the center. Place the bangle onto the circle and mark with a scribe the exact spots where the drawn lines meet the bangle.

13 Drill holes on the four marks equally spaced around the bangle: These will become the positions where the domes will be soldered. These holes will allow air to be released during soldering.

14 Taking your pre-cut ¼ in- (6mm) diameter disks, anneal and form them on a doming block.

15 Sand down in a figure eight on coarse emery paper to flatten and neaten up the base of each dome.

16 Fit the domes onto the four marked positions on the bangle. Using a half round needle file, file both the bangle and the domes until they fit neatly and accurately together for soldering.

17 Coat the bangle in flux, paying close attention to previous solder joins. Position the bangle in an upright position on a firebrick and hold in place with T-pins. Make sure the bangle is positioned with the first hole on a horizontal plane at the top.

18 Paint flux onto the first dome and position it onto the top drilled hole position. Place snippets of medium silver solder on the edge between the bangle and the dome, touching both.

19 Heat with a medium-sized flame, allowing the top half of the bangle and the area surrounding the dome to be heated before placing the flame onto the seam area. As solder flows, guide it around the dome by circling with the flame. Allow the bangle to cool before quenching and placing in pickle solution.

20 Once the bangle has been cleaned, flux and reposition, with the second drilled hole at the top. Hold it in place with the pins. Place the next dome on top and solder. Repeat this process on the remaining domes until all four have been successfully soldered. Allow to cool before quenching and immersing in pickle solution.

21 To flatten the top surface of each dome, use half D-section and half flat parallel pliers. Insert the curved D-section arm inside the bangle and apply the flat arm to the top of the dome. Hold and compress downward until a slight flat edge has been created on the dome. Repeat for the remaining three domes.

22 Remove any excess metal on the top and base of the bangle with a large flat file. File until the edge of the border and the internal bangle section meet flush and neatly together. Tidy up with emery sticks and various grades of emery paper.

23 To clean the inside of the bangle and the solder seam, use "D-shaped" files and emery sticks. Marks, excess solder, and fire-stain on the piece should be removed with various grades of emery paper. Take care not to remove or damage the edges of the bangle.

24 Polish on mops then immerse in liver of sulfur to blacken. Once the bangle has been blackened, remove the black by polishing on mops. This will leave a highly polished piece with blackened areas in the difficult-to-reach areas. Place the bangle in a solution of water and bicarbonate of soda, and boil for 5–10 minutes to remove the acidic pickle solution in the domes.

Spherical Cufflinks

This simple but attractive cufflinks design will allow you to learn how to create an "enclosed" piece of jewelry safely—with the addition of discreetly hidden air holes.

Jewelry pieces created from formed parts allow tactile 3D forms to be made. These forms can be quite large, while remaining lightweight. However, during the soldering of a piece that is constructed from enclosed parts, air will become trapped internally unless air holes are made. Not doing so could cause the pressure from the trapped air to explode the piece. A design produced for enclosed formed parts calls for discreet openings that are concealed by other components or that become a feature of the piece—perhaps a pierced pattern or another design feature that is in line with the architecture of the piece.

TOOLS AND EQUIPMENT

* Piercing saw
* Large flat file
* Doming block and punches
* Selection of emery papers
* Scribe
* Hand drill and ⅝ in (1.4mm) drill bit
* Borax cone, dish, and brush
* Hard and medium silver solder
* Binding wire
* Round nose pliers
* Metal ruler
* Dividers
* Selection of needle files
* Ring mandrel
* Rawhide mallet
* Stainless steel pins
* Reverse-action tweezers
* Emery papers and sticks

SKILL LEVEL ⚭

TECHNIQUES USED

* Multiple solder joins
* Sweat soldering
* Soldering a hollow form

MATERIALS:

Domes

4 silver disks of ¾ in- (19mm) diameter and ¹⁄₃₂ in (0.9mm) thickness

Textured wire pieces

3 x ⅛ x ¹⁄₃₂ in (75 x 4 x 1.6mm) length of rectangular wire to create a pair of ¾ in (18mm) lengths. Additional length is for holding while the texture is applied.

Fittings

2 x bought cufflink T-bars

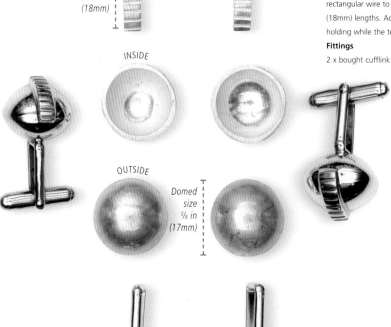

¾ in (18mm) · ⅛ in (4mm) · INSIDE · OUTSIDE · Domed size ⅝ in (17mm)

1 Measure four ¾ in- (19mm) diameter discs from ¹⁄₃₂ in (0.9mm) thickness of silver and cut out using a piercing saw. File with a large hand file until the edges are uniform and the pieces are completely round. Anneal the disks and place them individually in a doming block. Begin with a larger dome and work down to ⅝ in (17mm) diameter.

2 Once the correctly sized domes have been created, place each one separately onto coarse emery paper and sand down in a figure eight movement until the bases are flat. Check that the two pairs fit accurately together to form a rounded, flat bead shape.

3 Mark with a scribe and drill a hole in the center of two of the domes from inside. This will allow air to be released during the soldering process. The position of these holes can be discreetly hidden by the T-bar cufflink fitting at a later stage in the construction.

4 Place two of the domes upside down and flux their edges, then heat gently with a medium reducing flame before applying small paillons of flux-coated hard silver solder onto the edge. The solder will adhere to the slightly heated dome. Then apply heat from a medium neutral flame until solder runs. Allow to cool; then place in pickle solution to clean off excess solder and flux marks.

Tip

Prior to applying solder to difficult areas of soldering, flux and heat the area with a gentle flame. Cut solder paillons into a flux dish and, using tweezers, place the fluxed paillons on the heated area. The flux will adhere to the heated area and the solder paillons will stick easily and be held in position ready for soldering.

5 File or sand with coarse emery paper the edges of the two sweat-soldered domes to ensure a good fit with the matching domes. Position the flux-coated matching dome with the air hole on top and secure it with binding wire using round nose pliers. Direct heat around both domes with a medium-sized neutral flame, creating even heat distribution until the seam runs evenly with solder. Repeat with the second dome pair. Allow both to cool before removing the binding wire and placing in pickle solution.

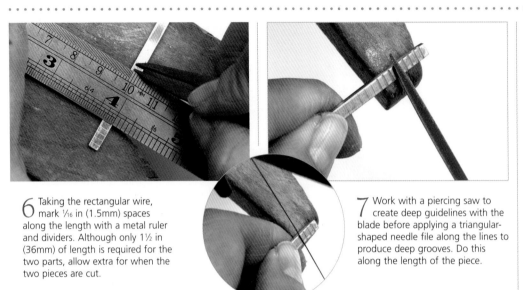

6 Taking the rectangular wire, mark 1/16 in (1.5mm) spaces along the length with a metal ruler and dividers. Although only 1½ in (36mm) of length is required for the two parts, allow extra for when the two pieces are cut.

7 Work with a piercing saw to create deep guidelines with the blade before applying a triangular-shaped needle file along the lines to produce deep grooves. Do this along the length of the piece.

8 Once the metal wire has been marked with the grooves, anneal the piece and hammer it around a ring mandrel. Hammer at the lower end, which has the larger circumference, matching the curve of the dome shapes. Check the curved piece against the dome to ensure the fit is tight and accurate. Re-anneal and hammer to fit if this is required.

9 Once the curve fits perfectly above the dome, position it. One end of the piece should sit approximately 1/8 in (4mm) over the dome center point; the other end should be flush to the end of the cufflink. Use a scribe to mark this point.

10 Cut at the scribe mark with a piercing saw. Repeat this process for the second piece and again saw off to fit the second dome shape.

11 File and fit the piece to the spherical dome using the flat side of a needle file. Make sure the curved wire fits as flush as possible, as any gaps will be difficult to solder.

12 Paint flux onto the dome and position it on a firebrick, with the dome at a slight angle, held in place with a stainless steel pin below. This will steady and keep the piece in position. To prevent solder from falling or being blown off, flux and heat the piece slightly before applying fluxed solder paillons on the joins on either side. This will allow the solder snippets to adhere.

13 Heat with a medium-sized neutral flame, concentrating the heat on the domed piece first, which will take longer to heat. Once it does, allow the flame to heat the rectangular wire. Once solder is flowing visibly on both sides, remove heat and allow to cool before quenching and placing in pickle solution.

14 Drill a hole on the top of the cufflink fittings, as this will allow the air hole to remain uncovered when the fitting is soldered to the domed parts.

15 File the top of the domes to allow a flatter surface to match and fit the cufflink fittings.

16 Coat the first dome piece with flux and place on the brick with a pin inserted beneath to steady and hold the rounded base in place. Paint flux onto the base of the cufflink fitting and position it, holding it in place with reverse-action tweezers. Add a small paillon of solder to the seam on one side, touching both the fitting and the domed part.

17 Steady the reverse-action tweezers with a prop such as a stainless steel pin if necessary. Before soldering begins, check that the drilled hole on the cufflink fittings is in line with the hole on the domed piece.

18 Heat with a medium-sized flame, concentrating first on the dome and then the top of the dome, before bringing flame to the base of the cufflink fitting. Circle the flame around the seam area. As the solder flows, remove the heat.

19 Clean any excess solder with a selection of needle files, emery papers, and sticks. Take care not to overfile the curve of the dome. Once all the fire-stain and marks have been removed, polish on mops until a mirror finish is achieved.

With holes discreetly in place, this formed pair of cufflinks give the appearance of a completely enclosed piece. Furthermore, when the cufflinks are worn on the sleeve, the holes become hidden.

Open-Bezel Locket Pendant

This design is a modern version of the traditional locket that can house personal objects such as a photograph, lock of hair, medicine, or perfume.

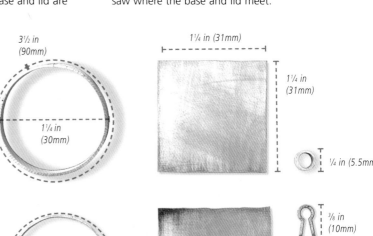

TOOLS AND EQUIPMENT
* Round mandrel
* Rawhide mallet
* Half-round ring pliers
* Borax cone, dish, and brush
* Hard and medium silver solder
* Selection of needle files
* Dividers
* Metal ruler
* Saw and fine blade
* Large flat file
* Coarse emery paper
* Stitching tool
* Reverse-action tweezers
* Emery papers

SKILL LEVEL ÖÖÖ

TECHNIQUES USED
* Using stitches
* Butt soldering
* Soldering jump rings
* Sweat soldering
* Soldering a hollow form

W̲ith modern methods of storing photographs, perhaps the attraction to lockets is no longer as great as it once was. However, container types of jewelry are tactile pieces that make charming gifts. The techniques learned from this project will allow you to develop and construct more commonly used, modern-day, boxlike objects such as lip balm containers, USB stick holders, or business card cases, to name but a few.

With this project, the box is constructed from one piece and then cut into two with a piercing saw. This method ensures the base and lid are exactly the same size and shape. The internal bezel is then fitted inside and secured with stitches. Fitting an internal bezel offers a good method of securing the lid without having to make a hinge and clasp system. This locket requires the soldering of a hollow construction. As with any hollow piece, an air hole must be created to allow the air to escape and prevent explosion of the pieces. To do so, a small incision is created with a piercing saw where the base and lid meet.

MATERIALS:

Base and top
2 pieces of 1¼ x 1¼ x ¹⁄₃₂ in (31 x 31 x 0.7mm) silver sheet

Sides
3½ x ¼ x ¹⁄₃₂ in (90 x 7 x 0.7mm) silver sheet

Internal bezel
3¼ x 1½ x ¹⁄₃₂ in (86 x 3.5 x 0.5mm) silver sheet

Keyhole detailing
½ x ¼ x ¹⁄₃₂ in (12 x 6 x 0.5mm) silver sheet

Pendant bale
⅛ in (3mm) of ¼ in (5.5mm) outer-diameter round silver tube

3½ in (90mm)

1¼ in (30mm)

3¼ in (86mm)

1¼ in (31mm)

1¼ in (31mm)

¼ in (5.5mm)

³⁄₈ in (10mm)

¼ in (5.5mm)

1 Take the 3½ in (90mm) length of annealed silver sheet and form it into a circle around a round mandrel with a rawhide mallet. Manipulate the ends with your hands or half-round ring pliers until they meet tightly.

2 Paint borax flux onto the ring, paying close attention to the seam. Put fluxed solder along the top of the seam and place onto a firebrick.

3 Heat the piece gently with a medium-sized neutral flame to allow the flux to dry, then concentrate heat on the opposite side to the seam so the expansion of the metal pushes the seam tighter together. Heat the piece until it starts to change to a dull red color, then place heat onto the area surrounding the seam. As soon as solder runs, withdraw the heat and allow it to cool before quenching in water. Place in pickle solution, wash, and dry.

4 Take one of the square pieces of silver, paint it with flux, and position it on a firebrick. Place the pre-soldered and cleaned ring in the center. Place paillons of hard silver solder on the outside edge, as this positioning will allow excess solder to be cleaned and removed.

5 Heat with a medium neutral flame. First concentrate on the base, allowing this part to heat, before moving onto the ring. Using the flame, circle around the outside and the inside of the seam. Once solder runs, continue using the flame to guide it all the way around the seam. When solder has flowed evenly, remove the flame.

6 When the piece is cooled and no longer glowing, quench, pickle, and wash. File and neaten the top edge if required. Once the top is level, use a divider and metal ruler to mark ⅛ in (3mm) down from the top edge all the way around the ring.

7 With a saw and fine blade, cut a gap into the side of the ring by following the scribed line. Only a small air hole is required to allow trapped air to escape during the soldering process, so, as soon as the blade pierces through, approximately ½ in (14mm) of the way around, stop sawing.

8 Coat flux onto the soldered piece and the second silver square. Place the square piece onto the firebrick and put the soldered piece facing downward on top. Lay snippets of fluxed hard silver solder along the base seam.

9 With a medium-sized neutral flame, heat the top and base piece before positioning the heat around the base sheet and the ring. As the two parts reach optimum temperature, a dull red in color, circle the flame around the seam area. As solder flows, guide it around the seam; then withdraw the heat when solder has run evenly.

10 Allow to cool for around one minute, until it is no longer glowing, then quench, pickle, and clean. Then saw the piece into two by following the scribed line, starting from the original pierced line. As you pierce with the saw, follow the line as close as possible to create a straight path.

11 When the two pieces have been cut and pulled apart, use a large flat file to even the top edges of what are now the base and lid of the pendant. With the ring section facing downward, sand the top and base in a figure eight on coarse emery paper. This will produce an even and flat edge.

12 With a saw, remove the excess metal from the corners of the top and the base. Do not take the blade right to the edge of the ring. As there will be further soldering, a slight edge should be maintained to allow solder to flow when the pieces are heated later and also to allow any slight movements during the further soldering process.

13 Taking the hand-pierced "keyhole" detailing, sweat solder onto the back. Flux the top and seam of the pendant lid and the "keyhole" detail. Place the keyhole detail onto the center of the lid with the solder facing downward.

14 Set the torch to a medium-sized neutral flame and heat the entire piece before focusing the flame on the top surface. As the piece starts to heat and turn dull red, look for the solder flow from the side of the keyhole detail.

15 Using a half round nosed needle file, shape and groove the top of the ring edge on the base of the pendant piece. This will allow a fingernail to be applied to pull the base from the lid when the two are fitted together.

16 Use dividers to draw an internal line on the base, measuring $\frac{1}{32}$ in (0.8mm) from the top edge. This line will be where the internal bezel will be soldered.

17
Taking a sharp stitching tool, create four stitches equally spaced around the ring on this scored line. The four stitches will hold the internal bezel in the correct position and secure it during soldering.

18 Using a ring mandrel and pliers, shape and form the ⅛ in (3.5mm) width of sheet silver for the internal bezel. Flux the bezel and place a snippet of hard solder onto the top of the seam. Place on a firebrick and heat with a medium-sized neutral flame.

19 Coat the internal bezel and the base of the pendant with flux. Put the bezel in position. Place paillons of hard silver solder on the inside of the seam, underneath the bezel so the solder flows up between the bezel and the pendant base. Do not place solder on the outer seam, as any excess solder will prevent the lid from sitting flush with the base.

20 Heat with a neutral flame, ensuring the base is heated first. Then concentrate on the seam area, using a turntable to view the inside. As even solder flow is achieved, withdraw the heat. Then cool, quench in water, and immerse in pickle solution.

21 File a groove into the top of the pendant base with a round needle file. This will allow the tube bale to sit flush and create a larger solder surface area. Solder next to or on top of the original seam, so all the joins are kept together, and cleaning and finishing are kept to the same area.

22 Paint flux onto the base, covering its entire surface, to prevent excess build-up of fire-stain and to allow an optimum surface for pre-soldered joins if they re-melt. Position and hold the fluxed tube in place with reverse-action tweezers. Place snippets of medium silver solder on the top, between the pendant base and the tube.

23 Heat the entire piece with a medium-sized neutral flame, then concentrate around the seam and surrounding area. Move the flame back and forth around this area until the solder flows. Allow to cool until no longer glowing before quenching in water and placing in pickle solution.

24 Once both pieces have been washed, file the edges of the base and lid until these are flush with the sides. If you find the base and lid do not fit perfectly, file the internal bezel slightly. Clean with emery papers, removing fire-stain and solder marks, before polishing with mops.

Moveable Ring

A wearer instinctively touches, twiddles, and spins their jewelry. This playful ring engages with the tactile nature of jewelry by bringing movement into the design itself.

TOOLS AND EQUIPMENT
* Ring mandrel
* Rawhide mallet
* Parallel pliers
* Borax cone, dish, and brush
* Hard and medium silver solder
* Handheld drill
* $\frac{1}{16}$ in (2mm) drill piece
* $\frac{1}{32}$ in (1mm) burr piece
* Reverse-action tweezers
* Round and half round needle files
* Burnisher
* Rouge powder and brush
* Soft-bristle wash brush
* Emery paper and files

SKILL LEVEL ♂♂

TECHNIQUES USED
* Soldering cast pieces
* Soldering wire
* Multiple solder joins

There are a number of methods for bringing movement into a piece of jewelry: for example, the use of a hinge, the inter-locking method, or as illustrated in this project, a "central bar thread through" system can offer a revolving mechanism. To allow the piece to function correctly, parts have to be protected with solder inhibitor during soldering to prevent solder flowing into unwanted areas of the piece. The main body of this piece has been cast to further enhance its tactility. Although

MATERIALS:

Ring shank
2¼ in (59mm) of ¼ x ⅛ in
(5.7 x 2.5mm) D-section silver wire

Internal bar
⅛ in (5mm) of ⅛ in (3mm)
round silver wire

Base tube
⅛ x ⅛ in (3.5 x 5mm) outer wall and
⅛ in (3.5mm) internal wall silver tube

Stone setting
⅛ x ⅛ in (2.5 x 5mm) outer wall and
⅛ in (3mm) internal wall silver tube
⅛ in (4mm) round faceted stone

Cast silver piece

casting can offer a wonderful array of shapes and forms, home casting can pose some problems during the soldering process. Solder has a tendency to run excessively into the holes of porous castings. Furthermore, due to the organic shapes and forms achieved from casting, components can be more difficult to set up and may prove to be more challenging to fit together for soldering. Soldering jigs and positioning tools will assist in the set-up.

Note

The cast piece applied in this ring was designed and produced with a CAD (computer-assisted design) casting system. However, if you wish, you can cast your own design using a sand casting clay system (see page 127), cuttlefish, or precious metal clay options. Alternatively, an independent jewelry casting company is able to cast from designs and drawings. Another option is to substitute the cast part of this project with a fabricated component.

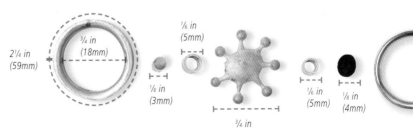

2¼ in (59mm) ¾ in (18mm) ⅛ in (3mm) ⅛ in (5mm) ¾ in (20mm) ⅛ in (5mm) ⅛ in (4mm)

1 Taking the D-shaped wire, anneal, form, and shape around a ring mandrel with the curved side of the "D" facing inward. This creates a rounded, softer, heavyweight but flat ring. Use a rawhide mallet and a pair of parallel pliers to manipulate the ends until these are straight and tight fitting.

2 When the ends meet perfectly, paint flux onto the ring and place flat onto a firebrick. Place a snippet of hard silver solder on the seam inside the shank.

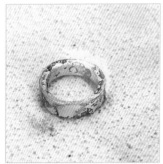

3 Heat the entire ring with a medium-sized neutral flame, then concentrate on the seam and the surrounding area. Cool for at least one minute, until no longer glowing, quench, pickle, and wash.

4 Using a 1⁄16 in (2mm) drill piece, create a depression in the center of the top of the ring. Then burr into the hole until it is fractionally bigger than the wire. This will allow the 1⁄8 in (3mm) wire to slot in and sit securely in place.

5 Paint flux onto the ring and the wire piece, paying close attention to the indentation before inserting the two together. Place the ring upright, supported with reverse-action tweezers. Place a small paillon of hard solder on the seam, touching both the wire and the ring.

6 Using a medium neutral flame, heat the ring first, then focus the flame around the seam area. Continue to move the flame, circling around the seam area until solder flows evenly. Allow to cool until no longer glowing—at least one minute. Quench, pickle, and wash.

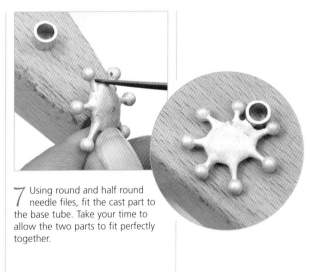

7 Using round and half round needle files, fit the cast part to the base tube. Take your time to allow the two parts to fit perfectly together.

8 Once a good tight fit has been achieved between the tube and cast part, apply a burnisher. With forward movements, close and cover any pit holes that may draw in excess solder.

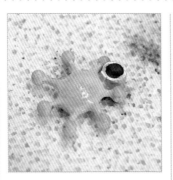

9 Coat both parts with flux and then position the cast piece on the firebrick. Place the fluxed tube in position before putting a snippet of hard silver solder on the seam, touching the cast piece and the tube.

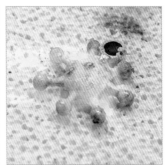

10 Heat with a medium-sized neutral flame. Heat the cast piece first. When the cast piece starts to become hot, heat the tube and the surrounding seam area. Once soldered, allow to cool for at least one minute, until no longer glowing, quench, and pickle.

11 Paint rouge paste onto the solder seam between the ring shank and the upright wire piece. Do not cover the top of the wire and leave approximately 1/16 in (2–2.5mm) at the end. This area must be free of solder inhibitor.

12 Paint rouge paste inside the tubing and the solder seam of the cast piece and then allow both parts to dry.

13 Hold the ring in place on the firebrick with reverse-action tweezers. Insert the cast part by threading the tube onto the wire of the ring shank.

14 Put on the top stone setting section, which should sit very tightly to the wire. Leave a very slight gap between the base tube and this stone setting to allow the cast piece to rotate freely. Carefully, using a small amount of flux, paint inside the tube.

15 Place a small paillon of medium silver solder inside the stone setting, touching the internal wall and the wire underneath.

16 Adjust the torch to a medium-sized neutral flame. Concentrate the heat around the top section of the ring and the cast component, as well as the tube area. As these areas start to change in color to dull red, circle the flame onto the tube and seam area. To view the solder running, you must look into the tube area.

17 Once the piece has been soldered successfully, allow it to cool until it is no longer glowing and then quench in water before cleaning the rouge with water and a soft-bristle wash brush. Remove all of it before placing in pickle solution.

18 Clean any excess solder or marks with files and emery paper before removing metal from the inside of the stone setting with a burr. This will create a seat and a tight fit to house the stone.

19 Clean the piece and set the stone before giving the piece a final polish.

Sand casting

Specially prepared sand or clay can be used to make an impression mold of an object; when molten metal is poured in, a copy of the form is produced. A two-part aluminum frame is required for this technique.

1 Break up any lumps in the clay and pack into the half of the frame with a lip. Hammer the surface to compact it, add more clay, and level the top. Push the object into the clay and dust the surface with talcum powder. Place the top half of the frame in position, fill with clay, and compact it. Separate the two parts of the frame and carefully remove the object.

2 Use a knife to cut the pouring channel and a thin rod to poke holes for air vents. The air vents must not cross the channel. Ensure no loose clay is present in the mold, as it could end up in the molten metal. Heat the metal with a pinch of borax powder in a crucible. Keep the torch on the metal as it is poured into the frame.

3 Quench the frame in cold water before splitting it to remove the casting. Immerse the casting in pickle solution to remove the oxides and then cut off any excess metal from the form and clean it up.

Hinged Bangle

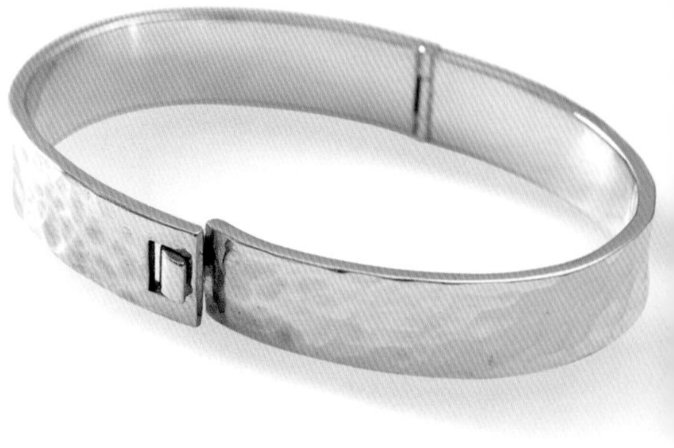

A hinged bangle is easy to get on and off, is secure to wear, and evenly balanced. A simple bangle design can be enhanced by a well-made hinge system.

TOOLS AND EQUIPMENT

- Planishing hammer
- Selection of needle files
- Oval bangle mandrel
- Rawhide mallet
- Round nosed pliers
- Dividers
- Metal ruler
- Piercing saw
- Reverse-action tweezers
- Borax cone, dish, and brush
- Hard silver solder
- Rouge powder and clean brush
- T-pin
- Graphic sticks
- Soft-bristle soft brush
- Emery papers and sticks
- Polishing mops
- Flat metal stake
- Rivet hammer

SKILL LEVEL ✶✶✶

TECHNIQUES USED

- Use of solder inhibitors

A hinge is a commonly used component for joining two pieces together while allowing movement between the parts. It is particularly useful for clasp mechanisms on jewelry pieces such as bangles, lockets, or torques, in addition to larger pieces such as card holders (see pages 146–150), or trinket boxes. Due to its movement and flexibility, a hinge is perfect for a piece—like a neckpiece or bracelet—that needs to sit flush against a curved neck or wrist. The designer may choose to make a feature of a hinge, or to disguise it.

A hinge is built from sections of tube called knuckles. These are interlocked with alternating pieces soldered to the separate sections. The interlocked knuckles are then joined and secured with a pin threaded through the center to allow the two or more pieces to move independently from each other. There must be a minimum of three knuckles and, ideally, an odd number should be applied so that both end knuckles are soldered to the same piece. This allows an even distribution of pressure from the internal pin and makes the hinge more secure and efficient.

As hinges are made from knuckles that must remain close but separate from each other, the soldering process can be tricky. If solder runs in between the three pieces, thus joining them, the hinge is unusable. Any excess solder may also hinder the usability of the hinge, so a solder inhibitor can be applied. Always give thought to the thickness of the tube and pin. Obviously, the heavier the weight of the piece, the thicker the tube and pin should be. In addition, the knuckles must sit aligned and as flush as possible to each other, so the central bar can be inserted. To ensure the pieces have been cut accurately, use a tube block if possible.

MATERIALS:

Bangle
7 x 3/8 x 1/16 in (180 x 10 x 2mm) silver rectangular wire (once hammered to create the textured surface you will need 3¼ in (86mm) and 3¾ in (96mm) lengths for the sides)

Outer knuckles
1½ in (40mm) of 1/8 in (2.4mm) outer- and 1/16 in (1.2mm) inner-diameter tubing (only ½ in /12mm required but the extra length is for holding the piece securely when working)

Central knuckle
1/6 in (5mm) of 1/8 in (2.4mm) outer- and 1/16 in (1.2mm) inner-diameter tubing

Central pin
¾ in (20mm) of 1/32 in (1mm) wire

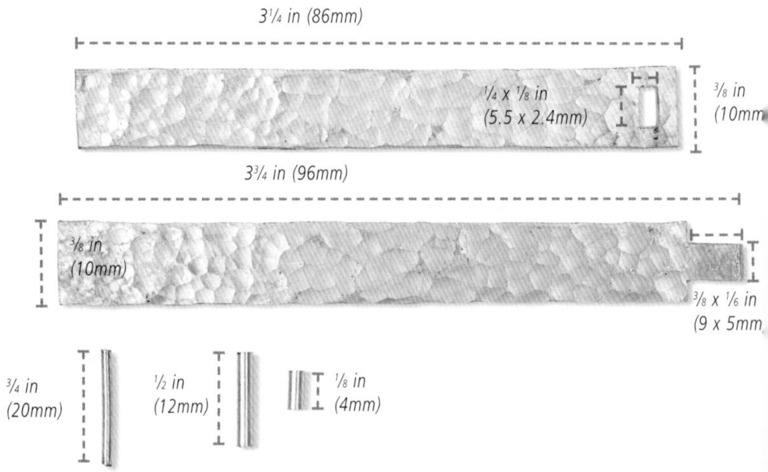
3¼ in (86mm)
¼ x 1/8 in
(5.5 x 2.4mm)
3/8 in
(10mm
3¾ in (96mm)
3/8 in
(10mm)
3/8 x 1/6 in
(9 x 5mm
¾ in
(20mm)
½ in
(12mm)
1/8 in
(4mm)

1 Hammer the length of the heavyweight wire with a planishing hammer to create the textured look. Pierce out the two pieces with a ¼ x ⅛ in (5.5 x 2.4mm) rectangular section cut out of the shorter piece and the ⅜ x ⅙ in (9 x 5mm) hook form on the end of the longer. File and make true before annealing and forming the heavy wires around an oval bangle mandrel with a rawhide mallet.

2 Once both sides of the bangle have been formed, fashion the hook with round nosed pliers. Bend and shape an outward curve. Do not worry too much about the shape, as this can be manipulated and adjusted when the two parts have been joined together.

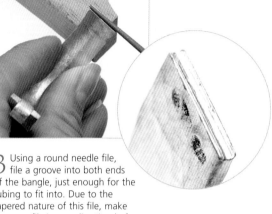

3 Using a round needle file, file a groove into both ends of the bangle, just enough for the tubing to fit into. Due to the tapered nature of this file, make sure you file in one direction before turning the piece over and filing from the opposite end. This will ensure that an even grooved area is achieved.

4 Using the 1½ in (40mm) piece of tubing, mark with dividers and a metal ruler a ½ in (12mm) length. Then, mark ⅛ in (4.2mm) inward on either side of this ½ in (12mm) length. This will create a central section measuring ⅛ in (3.6mm).

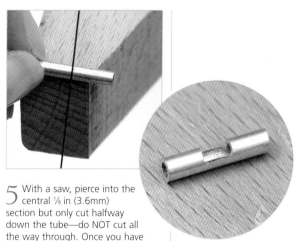

5 With a saw, pierce into the central ⅛ in (3.6mm) section but only cut halfway down the tube—do NOT cut all the way through. Once you have successfully removed the top section of the tube, cut it to the ½ in (12mm) length.

6 Take the half section of bangle with the pierced hole, cover with borax flux, and position on a firebrick. Hold the piece upright with reverse-action tweezers. Paint flux on the tube piece, with the removed section facing downward onto the groove at the bangle end that you created in step 3. Set small solder snippets on the inside of the bangle, on either side of the tube. Make sure the solder touches both the tube and the bangle.

7 Heat the piece with a medium-sized neutral flame. With the torch, follow the curve of the bangle, heating the main piece and then, once it starts to change in color to dull red, focus around the tube and the surrounding area. When solder flows, remove the heat and allow to cool for at least one minute before quenching and immersing in pickle solution.

8 With dividers, mark ⅛ in (3.9mm) in from each edge at the soldered end of the bangle to leave a central section of ⅛ in (4.2mm). Cut away this middle section of the tube with a piercing saw. This space will be for inserting the middle knuckle of the hinge.

9 File and work the inside of this area and the third knuckle so they fit snugly together.

10 Take time to fit both to ensure you don't overfile and make the hinge too loose. Each knuckle should measure approximately ⅛ in (4mm) long.

11 Using rouge solder inhibitor (a mixture of rouge powder and water), paint onto the previous soldered sections of tubing and the bangle, as well as the inside of the gap. This will prevent solder from running into the two knuckles, or in between the two bangle sections; in addition, it will prevent the previous solder join from reflowing and moving. Allow the rouge mixture to dry before linking this section of the bangle to the other side.

12 Carefully paint flux on the central knuckle on the side touching the bangle section with no soldered parts. Position the two bangle sections together and place a stainless steel T-pin beneath the knuckle soldered bangle side to support and hold the two pieces at the same level. Place graphic sticks through the center of the three knuckles to hold the pieces in place. Place solder paillons on the seam of the central knuckle on the inside of the bangle. Placing the solder here will allow any excess to flow inside instead of covering the textured outer surface.

13 Heat both sections of the bangle with a medium to large neutral flame to create an even and consistent heat. Once the bangle starts to change color to dull red, hold the flame around the area of the three knuckles. Concentrate on the central knuckle and the surrounding area; then, as solder flows, withdraw the heat.

Note

Graphic sticks have been inserted to keep the three knuckles in line with each other. As these are a nonmetal material and heat resistant, they are ideal. However, stainless steel wire can do the same job. If you use a stainless steel rod, ensure that it is not too tight a fit as there is a risk of it soldering to the knuckles. To prevent this from happening, apply a coating of rouge to the rod and allow it to dry before inserting it.

14 Once the parts are cooled, pull the two sections apart, which will reveal one side of the bangle with two soldered knuckles and the other with a central matching knuckle. Clean in soapy water with a soft-bristle soft brush before immersing in pickle solution. Remove any excess solder and marks with needle files and emery papers and sticks.

15 Once the bangle has been cleaned on mops to a mirror finish, link the two pieces together at the hinge by threading wire through. The wire should be longer than the hinge and, once threaded, any excess can be pierced off, leaving approximately 1/32 in (1mm) excess at the top and bottom.

16 Rivet the hinge by tapping the top and bottom on a flat metal stake with a rivet hammer. Tap the top to spread the metal wire, then flip the bangle over and repeat on the opposite end of the wire. Give the hinge part and bangle a final polish after riveting.

Tip

Make sure the central pin that is riveted is a tight fit to ensure the most secure and strongest of hinges.

The hook clasp on this bangle works with the hinge to create an attractive and secure method of fastening the piece.

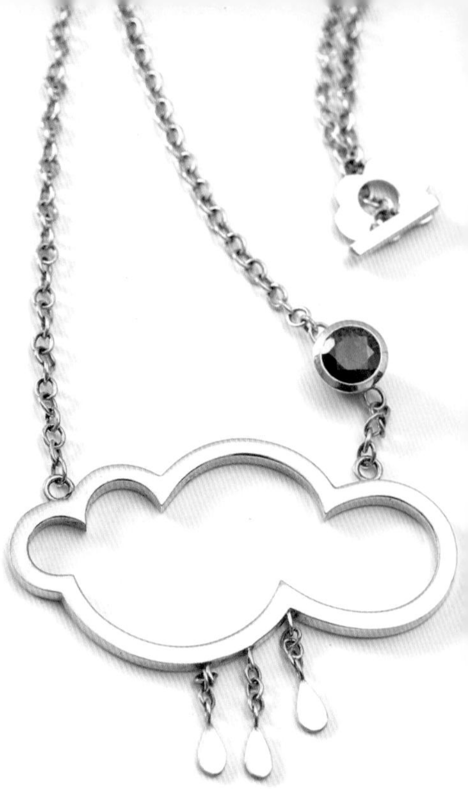

Come Rain or Shine Necklace

This pretty necklace design involves a number of different soldering techniques, which will put into practice much of what you have already learned: from soldering a bezel setting to soldering chain.

TOOLS AND EQUIPMENT

- Ring mandrel
- Rawhide mallet
- Half round ring pliers
- Scribe
- Piercing saw
- Selection of needle files
- Borax cone, dish, and brush
- Liquid flux and clean brush
- Hard silver solder
- Reverse-action tweezers
- Shears or wire snips
- Flat nosed pliers
- Long nosed pliers
- Emery papers and sticks
- Large polishing mops

SKILL LEVEL ✪✪✪

TECHNIQUES USED

- Soldering wire
- Multiple solder joins
- Soldering jump rings

The construction of this piece has been split into sections, with the main components made and soldered prior to the complete necklace being put together and joined. There are many solder joins, but, as most are spaced quite far apart, it is viable to use hard solder for as many joins as possible. The key to making the necklace successfully is to ensure that, when soldering the chain, you create an even temperature on the heavier parts before applying heat to the finer chain to prevent any melting.

MATERIALS:

Cloud form
8 in (200mm) of 1/8 in (2.5mm) square silver wire

Chain
15 3/4 in (400mm) of 1/8 x 1/8 in (3.5 x 2.6mm) trace chain

Cloud clasp and rain drops
5/8 x 5/8 x 1/32 in (17 x 17 x 1mm) silver sheet

T-bar clasp
1/2 in (14mm) of 1/16 in (2mm) square silver wire

Chain for rain drops
1 1/4 in (30mm) of 1/16 x 1/8 in (2.2 x 3.2mm) trace chain

Setting
1 x 1/4 x 1/32 in (24 x 6 x 0.7mm) silver sheet
4 x 1/8 in (4mm) jump rings made from 1/32 in (0.8mm) round wire
1/4 in (8mm) faceted stone

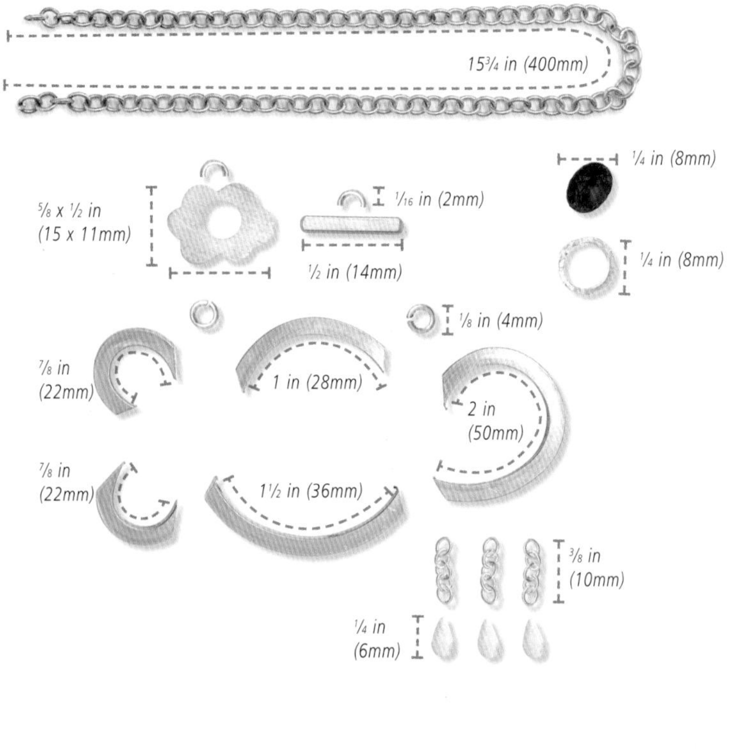
15 3/4 in (400mm)
5/8 x 1/2 in (15 x 11mm)
1/16 in (2mm)
1/2 in (14mm)
1/4 in (8mm)
1/4 in (8mm)
1/8 in (4mm)
7/8 in (22mm)
1 in (28mm)
2 in (50mm)
7/8 in (22mm)
1 1/2 in (36mm)
3/8 in (10mm)
1/4 in (6mm)

When making a necklace it is vital to think about how the piece will hang. In this project, the pendant, which suspends from a chain, has to sit flat against the skin as well as hang straight. The balance of the piece is important: If the piece is heavier on one side and the chain has not been soldered in a position to balance this, the main pendant will sit at an angle.

Consideration should also be given to the clasp and its position. The weight of the clasp must be relative to the piece. If the clasp is heavier than the main pendant, it will make its way to the front and end up hanging where the pendant should be.

A final point to remember is the length of the chain or neck piece. There are average lengths to work to, but with bespoke pieces of jewelry, each necklace can be manufactured to a personal length, allowing the main components to sit at a desired location. Be sure to link the pieces up and to wear them on your neck, checking the length, positions of components, and how the piece sits, before completing the soldering of the chain.

CLOUD FORM

1 Using annealed ⅛ in (2.5mm) square wire, form the first curved section of the cloud shape against a ring mandrel with a rawhide mallet. Use a piece of wire that is longer than required so you have enough to hold on to. Then manipulate and make the curve more pronounced with the help of a pair of half round ring pliers.

2 Check the curve against the drawing. Always use your designs and sketches as a template, then make copies and work from those so you are able to keep the original clean and safe.

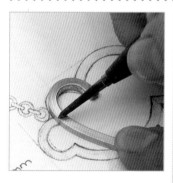

3 Place the curved wire piece against the drawing and, using a scribe, mark the end of the first curve.

4 Cut the curve at the scribed mark with a piercing saw before using a file to neaten the end. This will create the first curved section of the cloud.

5 Repeat the process until all the curved shapes have been formed and cut. Tidy the ends with a flat needle file.

6 Once all the parts have been finished, check that the pieces all fit well and correctly together and against the drawing.

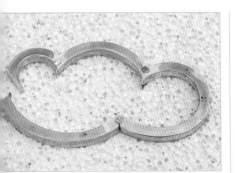

7 Paint borax flux on all the curved pieces except one and fit together onto a flat firebrick. Make sure the surface is even and flat so the pieces all sit perfectly in line. Apply hard silver solder to the top of each seam. Circle all the pieces with a medium-sized neutral flame to create even heat distribution. As each piece changes in color to dull red, concentrate the flame on the seams. When one seam solders, take the heat to the next until all have been soldered. Allow to cool for at least one minute, until no longer glowing, before quenching in water and immersing in pickle solution.

8 Once the piece has been cleaned, compare with the drawing and make any adjustments if required with a mallet against a ring mandrel, or manipulate with half round pliers. Once any adjustments have been made, fit the last curve. If necessary, file and fit. Compare with the drawing to ensure it matches perfectly.

9 Position the last curved piece and paint flux on the two joins as well as on the rest of the parts. Apply a paillon of solder on each join before heating with a medium-sized neutral flame. Distribute heat across the piece before focusing on the two new seams. As solder flows, remove the heat and allow the piece to cool naturally.

STONE SETTING

10 After the piece has been quenched in water, place in pickle solution. Clean any excess solder off with half round and round needle files. Place the piece on the drawing to establish the correct position for the jump rings. Using the round file, shape a slight groove on the sides of the cloud to allow the jump rings to fit.

11 Place the cloud form onto the drawing and mark the positions of the three drops. Scribe marks on the top and then the side of the wire. These marks will become the guidelines to solder raindrop chains from.

12 To make the stone setting, follow steps 5–8 in the "Bezel-Setting Ring" project on page 98. Then, taking the annealed bezel, insert it into a bezel block and hammer the punch with a rawhide mallet.

RAIN DROPS

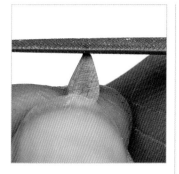

13 Using a piercing saw, scribe and cut three rain drop shapes from silver sheet. Use the flat end of a needle file to shape down a slight flat top to each of the drops. This will create a stronger and wider surface for the jump ring to solder to.

14 Place one rain drop piece onto a firebrick and position ⅜ in (10mm) of chain on the top. Coat the rain drop and the last jump ring with liquid flux. This type of flux does not expand so will work better to ensure the pieces do not move away from each other when heated.

15 Cut a minute piece of hard silver solder into a dish containing borax flux. As only a small amount of flux is used, expansion should be limited—but the wetness will help to secure the solder in place. Place the piece of solder on the join, touching both pieces.

16 Heat with a small neutral pencil flame, focusing first on the rain drop. As the pieces are small, the heating and soldering will occur almost instantly, so pay attention and work fast. As soon as the piece reaches a dull red color, stroke the flame over the jump ring and watch the solder flow before removing the heat. Repeat this process for the two remaining drops. Quench, pickle, and clean, before washing and drying off.

CLASP

17 Taking two of the pre-made jump rings, cut slightly less than half away and file the two ends of the remaining semicircles until both are the same length and flat.

18 Coat one of the half jump rings in borax flux and position onto the bar of the T-bar clasp. Secure the ring in position with reverse-action tweezers, which will also act as a heat sink, preventing the half jump ring from melting during the soldering process. Solder with a small, neutral pencil flame.

19 Repeat the half jump ring soldering process for the ring part of the clasp. Once both have been soldered, you will have these two ready for the next stage of linking the parts of the necklace together.

JOINING THE PARTS

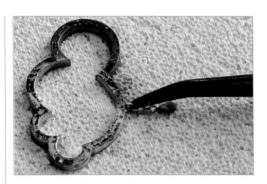

20 Coat the cloud piece and the last jump ring of each rain drop chain in borax flux. Take the first rain drop chain, holding the last jump ring of the chain with reverse-action tweezers. The tweezers will act as a heat sink. Apply a small paillon of solder, touching the jump ring and the cloud part.

21 With a small neutral flame, heat the cloud part. Once it starts to change to dull red in color, focus the heat around the solder seam area, keeping heat away from the chain for now. As the area of the cloud near the seam starts to get hotter, flick the flame over the jump ring just enough to allow the solder to run. As soon as solder has flowed, remove the heat immediately. Once the first rain drop chain has been soldered, allow the piece to cool for at least a minute, until no longer glowing, then quench and pickle. When the piece has been cleaned, flux again and repeat the process until all three drops have been successfully soldered.

Tips

• Liquid flux has been used only on very small, delicate parts as it is easier to apply without disturbing the set-up than thick borax flux and there is less chance of pieces moving when heated.

• When soldering the last two drops, ensure you coat the previous solder joins in flux. Additionally, set the torch to a small needle flame so you are able to direct and focus heat only on the chain you are working on.

• If, after soldering, the jump rings of the three chains are sitting uneven, straighten with pliers.

22 Paint the cloud pendant with borax flux, coating the entire piece and the previous joins. Take care to coat the pre-filed groove where the cloud and the jump ring meet (made in step 10). Coat the jump ring in flux and hold in place with reverse-action tweezers.

Tip

Take care when using reverse-action tweezers to hold jump rings or other delicately shaped parts. During soldering the heat can cause the piece to become distorted from the pressure of the tweezers. One way to avoid this problem is to melt the solder on the side of the cloud, while holding the jump ring at a close distance with tweezers. Then, as soon as the solder runs, swiftly move the jump ring into place and release the tweezers.

23 Heat the cloud pendant with a small neutral flame, concentrating on the area closest to the chain. As soon as the metal changes color to dull red, let the flame flick onto the jump ring, just enough for the solder to flow. Once the first jump ring has been soldered, cool, quench, and place in pickle solution before repeating the process for the second jump ring on the opposite side of the cloud.

24 Using shears or wire snips, cut your 15¾ in (400mm) chain in half. To make the necklace hang straight, make one length slightly shorter than the other so that once the diameter of the bezel setting is added to it, the two lengths are the same. Take the shorter length of chain and cut open the last link before linking up with the jump ring attached to the cloud part. Close the link with pliers.

25 Apply liquid flux and a small paillon of hard solder to the cut link and heat with a pencil flame. This will become hot extremely fast and solder very quickly. Remove the heat promptly to avoid melting the chain. Allow to cool for at least one minute before quenching and placing in pickle solution.

26 After the cloud piece has been cleaned, position over the drawing to determine the length of chain from which the stone setting will hang. Cut at the correct length with shears or wire snips.

27 Coat the stone setting and chain in liquid flux and set the pieces onto the firebrick. Position the chain so the last link is in contact with the stone setting. Place a minute snippet of solder onto the join.

28 Heat with a small neutral flame, concentrating on the setting first and, as soon as the color changes to dull red, allow the flame to flicker over the chain. Solder should flow immediately. Remove the heat and allow to cool before quenching and pickling. Repeat steps 27 and 28 to attach the remainder of this chain length to the opposite side of the setting.

29 After cleaning, use pliers to link the other end of the chain to the T-bar. Place solder on the join and heat with a small neutral flame until solder flows, joining the chain and T-bar together.

Tip

When soldering small parts with fine snippets of solder, to hold the solder in position and stop it from blowing away, first bring the flame gently around the surrounding area to heat the form and dry the flux. Do not direct the needle flame straight onto the solder or solder area to begin with.

30 Repeat steps 24 and 25 to attach the longer length of chain (created in step 24) to the jump ring on the opposite side of the cloud. Link the end of the second chain to the cloud-shaped toggle part of the clasp by cutting the last link on the chain with shears or snips. Close the link with pliers before applying liquid flux and a small snippet of hard silver solder to the seam.

31 Again, using a small neutral flame, solder the link closed. Allow the piece to cool before placing the necklace in water and then pickle solution.

32 Clean and remove any excess solder or marks with a selection of emery papers and sticks. Give a final polish with large motorized mop or handheld mops. Set the stone and give a finish polish over the setting.

Leaf Brooch

This is a simple brooch design with clean and sharp lines. Inlaying with a contrasting color of metal works beautifully to add visual impact to such a graceful and modest design.

TOOLS AND EQUIPMENT

* Scribe
* Piercing saw
* Selection of needle files
* Borax cone, dish, and brush
* Hard silver solder
* Metal ruler
* Double-sided tape
* Wooden board
* Scoring tool
* Flat nosed parallel pliers
* Stainless steel pins
* Hand drill and ⅛ in (1.5mm) drill bit
* Reverse-action tweezers
* Selection of emery papers and sticks

SKILL LEVEL ⭕⭕⭕

TECHNIQUES USED

* Scored and folded chamfered joins
* Soldering inlay
* Soldering of wire

Inlay works best when using highly contrasting colored metals. If you wish to use higher-value metals such as silver, gold, and platinum, look for the greatest color differences for maximum effect. For example, silver works best with higher-karat golds as they have the most contrasting color. Copper inlaid to silver could be patinated. This would offer an interesting and strong color contrast between the blue-green of the copper and the whiteness of the silver. Using a matte texture can also further highlight the color difference between two metals, as well as offering a soft and tactile feel. Remember that inlaying can offer a wonderful base sheet that can later be formed and fabricated into pieces.

MATERIALS:

Leaf shape
2¾ x 2 x ¹⁄₃₂ in (70 x 50 x 1mm) silver sheet

Copper inlays
⅝ x ½ x ¹⁄₃₂ in (15 x 12 x 1mm) copper sheet

Brooch
3¼ in (85mm) of ¹⁄₁₆ in (1.4mm) round silver wire
Pre-bought silver brooch pin protector

Ensuring pieces fit well together requires time and patience in the filing and fitting process. When you are filing, only carry out a couple of strokes at a time before checking the fit against the matching piece. If you rush through this step, you risk removing too much metal and making the piece too small to inlay accurately. Prior to working in high-value metals, make sure you are confident with the inlaying process. If you overfile a piece for fitting, then you have to start again, wasting the metal. It is best to start on lower-cost metals such as brass or copper with silver before progressing to more valuable metals.

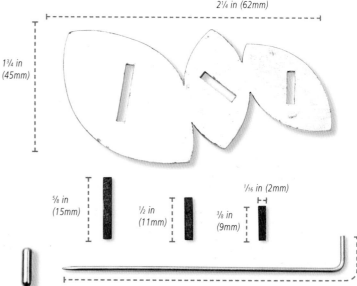

1 Taking the sheet of silver, scribe and cut the shape with a piercing saw. Once the sides have been filed and neatened with a file, mark and scribe the inlay sections before drilling ¹⁄₃₂ in (1mm) holes inside each. Pierce with a saw, carefully following the inside of the line to avoid removing excess metal.

2 Cut the copper pieces slightly big to fit the three inlays and then file to fit the gaps. Ensure that you take time when filing and only carry out a couple of strokes of the file prior to checking against the pierced area. This will avoid overfiling and making the pieces too small to fit.

3 Check that all three copper inserts fit perfectly and tightly into the pierced silver gaps. To check that the fit is accurate, hold the piece to the light. If the fit is good, there should be minimum light passing through the part.

Tip

Make sure the piece you are inlaying is pierced slightly larger than the piece that is housing the inlay. This means you have room to allow for filing and fitting of the inlay.

4 Paint flux inside the three pierced-out areas and the sides of the copper pieces, before inserting the parts together. Coat the piece with borax flux on the front and back surface. Turn the piece upside down and place onto a flat firebrick. Place small paillons of hard solder along the seams, making sure that they touch both metals.

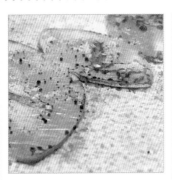

5 Heat the entire piece with a medium-sized neutral flame. Hold the flame back at first to allow the flux to dry and expand slowly before shrinking again. This will also prevent the solder from flying off. Once the flux is dried, bring the flame closer and move from the top edge of the piece, zigzagging down to the bottom edge.

6 Once the piece starts to heat and change in color to dull red, concentrate on each inlay. When each seam flows with solder, move onto the next inlay until all three have been successfully soldered. Do not worry about excess solder flooding the surface, as this can be filed and removed at a later stage.

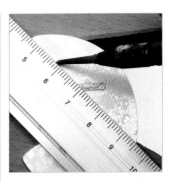

7 After the soldered piece has cooled for at least one minute, until it is no longer glowing, quench and place in pickle solution. Dry off and use a metal ruler and a scribe to mark a line down the center of each "leaf" shape on the back of the piece. Turn the piece over and also draw two lines on the join lines where the three leaf shapes meet.

8 Using double-sided tape, place and secure the piece, with the back facing upward, onto a wooden board. Begin scoring the first line using a metal ruler as a guide. Once a fine groove has been established, remove the ruler and continue along the line with greater force. Continue until you have removed approximately a third of the metal thickness. Repeat the process with the other two lines.

9 Carefully remove the piece from the board and flip over, then secure in place with double-sided tape. Repeat the scoring process on the two lines between the three leaf shapes.

10 Remove the piece from the board and anneal before lining up the top engraved line against the edge of the board. Push the fold against a stable support, such as the side of the bench.

11 Fold the other lines against the board with the assistance of flat nosed parallel pliers. Take care once the folds have been created that no further pressure is applied, as this can break the pieces off.

12 Coat the piece with flux. Place the piece on a firebrick with its back toward you and keep in an upright position with the help of stainless steel jewelry display pins. The pins will also prevent the folded parts from deforming. Place paillons of solder along the seams.

13 Heat with a medium-sized neutral flame. Zigzag the flame across the piece, allowing even distribution of heat. As the flux changes to a glassy appearance and the silver starts to darken in color, the solder will begin to flow. Direct the flow along the seams, one at a time. Once solder has flowed evenly across all three seams, remove the heat and allow to cool until no longer glowing.

14 After quenching and cleaning, turn the brooch over and place it on the firebrick. Paint flux onto the surface of the piece, paying close attention to the two seams. Place paillons of hard silver solder along the seams between the leaves. No pins have been applied to hold the piece in position as it is now partially soldered and more secure. However, if you feel it's necessary, pins can be applied.

15 Heat the entire piece with a medium-sized neutral flame. Then focus the flame around the seams and surrounding area. As solder flows, remove the flame, then allow the piece to cool for at least one minute before quenching and placing in pickle solution.

16 Drill a slight opening in the center-back of the largest outer leaf for the brooch pin, making sure the drill does not go all the way through the metal. Paint both sides of the piece with flux and place on the firebrick, supporting with stainless steel pins so it is in as horizontal a position as possible.

17 File the wire to a sharp point on one end and to a flat surface on the other end, which can be inserted into the drilled hole. Measure ⅜ in (10mm) from the flat end and bend with flat pliers into a 90-degree angle. Insert this short end into the hole and hold in place with reverse-action tweezers. Place a small snippet of solder on the end of the wire, touching the wire and the brooch.

18 Heat with a gentle neutral flame. Circle and focus the flame onto the brooch piece rather than the pin. Once the piece starts to turn dull red, flick the flame over the pin. Solder should run quickly. Remove the flame and cool for at least a minute, until no longer glowing. Quench and pickle.

19 Clean the piece with emery paper and sticks before polishing on mops. This cleaning and polishing process should also work-harden the pin, which will have become quite soft during soldering.

A DOZEN ROSES
SUZAN REZAC

This truly stunning neckpiece has been made from a selection of handmade beads. Each silver bead has been carefully inlaid and soldered before being colored to form this strong contrast of the black against the matte silver.

Pendant

This bail-free pendant is constructed using the investment soldering technique (see pages 80–81). Plaster is used to hold the pieces in place—stabilized, fitted, and aligned—during soldering.

TOOLS AND EQUIPMENT
- ★ Compass and set square
- ★ Paper or thin card
- ★ Masking tape
- ★ Investment plaster
- ★ Water
- ★ Measuring pitcher
- ★ Eggcup or other container
- ★ Ring mandrel
- ★ Rawhide mallet
- ★ Half round ring pliers
- ★ Borax cone, dish, and brush
- ★ Hard and medium silver solder
- ★ Protractor
- ★ Scribe
- ★ Round nosed needle file
- ★ Stainless steel tweezers
- ★ Selection of emery papers
- ★ 1/32 in (0.7mm) burr and hand drill

SKILL LEVEL ⚬⚬⚬

TECHNIQUES USED
- ★ Investment soldering
- ★ Multiple solder joins
- ★ Soldering wire
- ★ Soldering jump rings

Fabricating a pendant out of wire has the advantage of allowing you to create a sizeable but lightweight and comfortable piece. This design can be suspended at various angles by linking chain through different wire sections. The wearer can also adapt the piece by changing the component it suspends from, be it varying chains or cords, mixed and matched to the color of the stones. This pendant can also be worn on the wrist, wrapped with leather cord or chain. If you wish, you can add brooch fittings to the back and change this from a pendant to a brooch.

Multiple wire pieces can be difficult to construct due to the numerous solder joins and the complicated assembly. Not only does the set-up prove difficult but multi-solder-joined pieces pose the risk of previous joins opening during further soldering. Furthermore, wire is at risk of melting when exposed to soldering heat. Using plaster to stabilize the pieces, either by embedding pieces in the plaster (see pages 80–81) or by creating a prop out of plaster on which the pieces can sit securely (as in this project), not only ensures the security of parts but also means the difficult body of the piece can be soldered in one action rather than by the time-consuming and risky method of soldering each and every join separately.

Note

Investment plaster can be poured into any type of shaped container, allowing you many construction and soldering possibilities. Whatever form you decide to create, ensure you are able to remove the plaster from the mold to allow soldering access.

MATERIALS:

Outer ring
3½ in (90mm) of 1/16 in (2mm) round silver wire

Inner ring
1½ in (36mm) of 1/16 in (2mm) round silver wire

Wire design
7 x ½ in (14mm) of 1/16 in (2mm) round silver wire

Settings
3 pieces of ¼ in (8mm) x ¼ in (6mm) outer-diameter 1/8 in (4.3mm) inner-diameter silver tube
3 x 1/8 in (5mm) round faceted stones

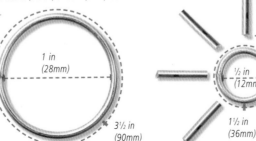

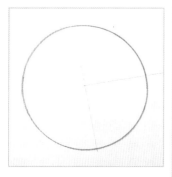

1 With a compass, measure and draw a circle with a diameter of 2 in (52mm) onto paper or thin card. Using a set square, mark a 90-degree angle.

2 Cut down one of the lines to the center and fold the cut line to the other line.

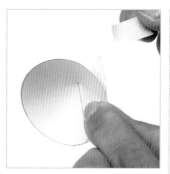

3 To create the cone, use masking tape to tape the edge closed.

4 Following the manufacturer's instructions, mix investment plaster with water in a plastic pitcher. Sit the cone in an upright position, held within an eggcup or similar item. Pour the mixture into the cone up to the top and leave to set.

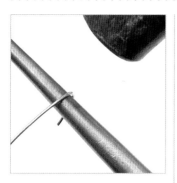

5 With a ring mandrel and rawhide mallet, shape and form the inner and outer rings for your pendant. Manipulate with half round ring pliers to make the ends meet together.

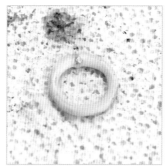

6 Flux the smaller ring and place flat onto a firebrick. Place a small paillon of hard silver solder onto the seam.

7 Heat the piece with a medium-sized neutral flame. Due to the size of the piece it will become heated quickly and soldering will occur relatively quickly. After soldering, cool for at least a minute until the metal is no longer glowing, quench, and place in pickle solution.

8 Repeat the soldering process for the larger ring. Once cooled, quench, place in pickle solution, and wash with water. Check that both rings are soldered correctly and reshape into a circle on a ring mandrel if necessary.

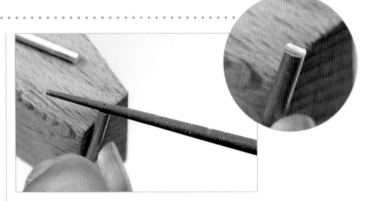

9 Draw a circle of 1¼ in (31mm) diameter and mark 45-degree angles before placing the larger ring on top. Use a scribe to mark the 45-degree angles onto the ring. These eight marks are now your guidelines for positioning the wire pieces.

10 Shape and fit the seven wire pieces onto the curve of the large ring. To do this, remove the paper from the plaster cone, turn it upside down, and slide the large ring onto it. You can now balance the wire pieces on the ring to make sure you get the placement, angle, and fit just right.

11 To ensure a good fit of the wire and the ring, using a needle file, file the bottom of each wire piece to create a curved groove which will fit neatly onto the curve of the large ring at each scribe mark. Every scribe mark, apart from one, should have a wire piece fitted to it.

12 Once all the pieces have been fitted onto the ring, place the plaster cone onto a firebrick and paint flux over the ring. Flux each wire piece and position onto the scribed marks where each has been filed to fit. Place a small snippet of hard silver solder where each wire piece touches the ring.

13 Set the torch to a medium-sized neutral flame and start to heat the ring. Circle the piece with the flame, using a revolving turntable to assist your view and access all areas. As the investment plaster absorbs heat, it will take some heat away from the piece, but continue to circle the piece until it starts to change to a dull red. Now focus the flame on each join. As a join becomes soldered, move onto the next until all seven have been soldered successfully.

14 Once the piece is soldered, remove from the cone with stainless steel tweezers and allow it to sit on another area of the firebrick to cool for at least one minute, until the metal stops glowing. Quench and pickle before turning it upside down. Place the smaller ring inside and use a scribe to mark where the seven wires touch the inner ring.

15 Take a round nosed needle file and remove a groove on each of the scribed marks so the ring can sit flush with the curve of each wire piece.

Tip

On each occasion that solder is heated, its melting point increases. This means that when you solder a piece with multiple solder joins, if you are skillful and quick, you should be able to do further soldering without the piece collapsing. However, if you wish to be cautious with the soldering of the second ring, you can cover the original solder joins with rouge powder mix or another type of solder/heat inhibitor.

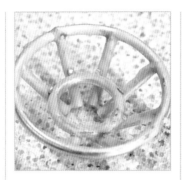

16 Place the smaller ring inside the piece, matching the seven grooves with the seven pieces of wire. Coat the parts with flux and place a small snippet of hard silver solder on each join.

17 Begin using a slightly softer reducing flame, allowing this to dry the flux and to prevent solder from flying away.

18 Adjust the torch to a medium-sized neutral flame and heat the internal ring and the wires surrounding where it is touching. As the piece starts to heat and change in color to dull red, focus the flame on each join. As one join becomes soldered, move onto the next until all have been completed. Allow the piece to cool: Do not quench.

19 After removing the piece from pickle solution, wash in clean water and place onto the firebrick. Cover the piece in flux and position the three settings on the large gap between the first and seventh wires. Heat slightly with a reducing flame before applying small snippets of medium solder to the joins. Solder should be applied to any points where two metals meet between the settings and the wires.

20 Turn the torch to a medium-sized neutral flame and heat the piece, concentrating the flame on the large ring and the three settings. Keep heat around the setting and the surrounding area. As one seam starts to solder, move the flame onto another until the seams and joins are all flowing with solder. Allow to cool for at least one minute, until no longer glowing, before quenching.

21 Place the piece in pickle solution, then wash. Once cooled and cleaned, check the soldering of the three pieces of tubing as it may take more than one attempt to solder these successfully. If required, apply additional solder to these areas and repeat step 17. Clean up any excess solder, marks, and fire-stain with a selection of emery papers. Use folded pieces of emery to get into difficult-to-reach areas.

22 Burr away metal inside each of the settings to create a seat for the stones. Polish the piece before setting the stones and giving a final polish on mops.

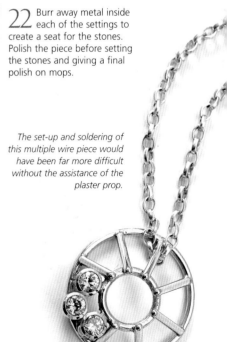

The set-up and soldering of this multiple wire piece would have been far more difficult without the assistance of the plaster prop.

Business Card Case

When you have mastered the basic skills of jewelry making, you may wish to progress to accessories, such as these business card holders—or money clips, tie clips, trinket boxes, or belt buckles.

TOOLS AND EQUIPMENT

* Dividers
* Double-sided tape
* Wooden board
* Metal ruler
* Scoring tool
* Center punch or scribe
* Piercing saw
* Large flat file
* Selection of small needle files
* Rawhide mallet
* Metal stake
* Three additional firebricks
* Borax cone, dish, and brush
* Hard silver solder
* Enamel mesh
* Emery paper and sticks

SKILL LEVEL

TECHNIQUES USED

* Scored and folded chamfered joins
* Sweat soldering

The soldering of larger items is similar to that of smaller jewelry parts, but more heat is required to achieve the optimum overall heat to allow the solder to flow. To assist with this, a wall of fire bricks can be constructed behind the soldering area, which will reflect some heat back onto the piece you are soldering. The heat from a small portable torch will not be sufficient for larger items, so make sure you use a suitable torch.

Always give consideration to the weight of an accessory during the design process. If you plan to make an item that, like this business card holder, has to be portable, take into account the weight of the metal. Reducing the amount of metal will make the product more cost-effective. However, remember that the metal must be sufficiently thick to be durable for the item's purpose. In this project, 1/32 in (0.9mm) thick metal has been used which makes the card case suitable for desk use. If you wish to carry this case, it would be best to use 0.7mm thick metal.

MATERIALS:

Body of case
2¾ x 3¾ x 1/32 in (70 x 93 x 0.9mm) silver sheet

Base of case
2⅜ x 3½ x 1/32 in (60 x 90 x 0.9mm) silver sheet

Top feature
1¼ in x ⅜ x 1/32 in (30 x 10 x 0.9mm) silver sheet

Tip

Try to ensure when you are soldering any piece—but especially an item with lengthy solder joins—that the seams are concealed as much as possible, perhaps at the item's back or base.

3¾ in (93mm)

2¾ in (70mm)

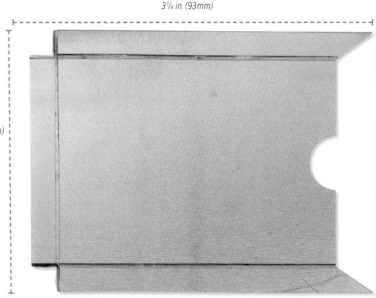

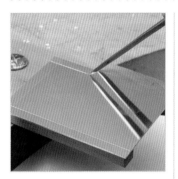

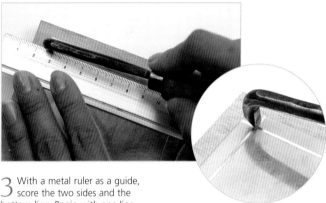

1 Take the 2¾ x 3¾ x ¹⁄₃₂ in (70 x 93 x 0.9mm) silver sheet and, using dividers, mark ¼ in (7mm) guidelines from the bottom edge and the two sides. These will become the lines to score and, once folded, the sides of the card holder.

2 Using double-sided tape, attach the sheet—with scored lines facing upward—to the center of the wooden board. This allows the piece to be held securely, as well as providing a stable grip during the scoring process.

3 With a metal ruler as a guide, score the two sides and the bottom line. Begin with one line, taking care and time to score lightly at first to avoid score marks going off the line. Once a slight indentation has been achieved and there is a more pronounced line to follow, apply greater pressure to remove more metal. Continue to score each of the lines until half the metal thickness has been evenly removed from all three.

Tip

When scoring and folding pieces, the jeweler should position themselves at a height where they feel comfortable and can bring to bear quite substantial force. Bear this in mind before you start.

3½ in (90mm)

2³⁄₈ in (60mm)

⅜ in (10mm)

⅜ in (10mm)

¼ in (7mm)

⅜ in (10mm)

⅜ in (9.5mm)

4 Using dividers, mark a line ⅜ in (10mm) in from the top edge. On this line, create a faint mark in the middle with a center punch or scribe.

5 Using this center mark as a guideline, scribe with the dividers a semicircle of ¾ in (19mm) diameter into the main section of the case.

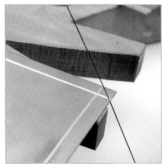

6 Remove the sheet of silver from the wooden board and carefully pierce and detach the two bottom corner squares created by the scored lines. You will also need to remove from the top a ⅜ in (10mm) strip, cutting a diagonal line from the top corners of the silver sheet to the top corners of the internal, scored rectangle. Finally, pierce and detach the semicircle.

7 With a large flat file, file and make all the edges true. Using a needle file, create a 45-degree angle on the two edges of the sides. When the three sides are folded, these filed and chamfered edges will meet perfectly into a right angle.

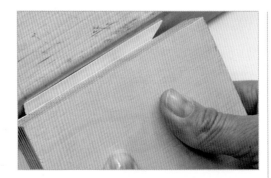
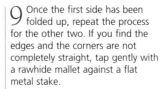

8 Anneal the sheet and place it on the wooden board with the first scored line against the edge of the board. Push the fold up against a support surface, such as the side of a workbench. This will allow you to apply even pressure, creating a neat fold.

9 Once the first side has been folded up, repeat the process for the other two. If you find the edges and the corners are not completely straight, tap gently with a rawhide mallet against a flat metal stake.

10 Once all three sides are straight and the ends are touching perfectly, flux the entire surface, paying close attention to the seams. Build an "oven" by placing three additional firebricks next to the sides and behind the firebrick to create an enclosed space. Place paillons of hard solder along the seams and at the corners.

Warning

When an "oven" is created, on occasion the flame can reflect and blow back in the direction of the jeweler. If you find this happening, remove one of the side bricks and place the parts for soldering at the other end. This will allow the flame reflection to exit away from you, but it will also enclose less heat so the soldering process may take longer.

11 Begin with a large reducing flame and heat the entire piece gently to allow the flux to dry and solder to adhere to its positions. Once the flux has dried, adjust the torch to a large neutral flame and circle around the entire piece. Due to the size of the piece, it will take time to heat sufficiently to allow solder to flow.

12 As the piece starts to heat up and change in color to dull red, concentrate the flame along the seams. Focus on the outside and the internal seam and, as the solder starts to flow, pull it along with the flame and ensure you heat the corners sufficiently to allow solder to flow upward on the channel.

13 Leave the piece until it is definitely cool and the metal has stopped glowing, before quenching in water and placing in pickle solution—if you are not patient you risk distorting the piece. As this piece is of a substantial size, the piece and surrounding area will take a longer time to cool, approximately 2–3 minutes, to be safe.

14 Use a large flat file to even the top edge of your card holder. Make sure this edge is straight, flat, and fits flush against the flat sheet of silver that will form the base of the case.

15 When the body of the card holder fits flush with the base sheet, flux the entire surface of both parts, paying close attention to the previous solder joins. Place the top onto the base within the "oven" area and position solder onto the outer edge along the seams.

16 Again, heat with a large, bushy reducing flame until the flux has dried and solder is secured firmly. Then increase to a neutral flame and circle around the entire piece, allowing equal heat distribution to both parts. Once both parts start to change to dull red, pull the flame back and forth along the seam. As solder flows, remove the heat. Cool for 2–3 minutes, quench, and pickle.

Tip

As this piece is of substantial size, it will take a lot of heat and time to heat evenly enough to allow solder to flow. You may find positioning the piece on top of wire mesh such as enamel wire will allow heat to filter underneath and evenly across the piece.

17 Take your three pre-pierced and engraved detailed pieces and sweat solder them before cleaning and removing excess solder with emery paper or files.

18 Coat the card holder in flux and then paint flux onto the sweat-soldered surface of the three detailed pieces. Position them on top of the card holder. To ensure the pieces are located correctly and evenly, measure the top of the card holder and mark with dividers the exact positions.

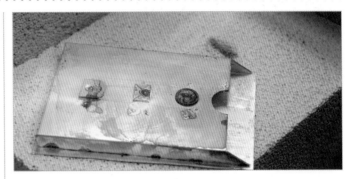

19 Heat the entire case with a large neutral flame and then concentrate on the main body. As the join is between the pieces and the body, an even heat must be maintained between the two. Once the piece starts to change to dull red, focus on the three detailed parts and the metal below. Circle the heat around each piece and, as solder flows, move onto the next piece until all three have been soldered successfully.

20 Once solder has flowed evenly on all three pieces, leave them to cool until the metal is no longer glowing before quenching and immersing in pickle solution. Do not place the piece in water until it has fully cooled—wait at least 2–3 minutes, until it is no longer glowing. If at all in doubt, wait longer. Having patience will allow you to avoid quenching the metal when it is too hot.

21 Dry off the piece and then remove the excess metal with a piercing saw. To cut a straight line from the top of the base, scribe a line with dividers from the edge of the two corners.

22 File with a large flat file, taking care to remove metal until the edges are flush and flat. Keep the file flat when filing to avoid removing sharp straight edges and corners.

23 Using varying grades of emery paper and sticks, sand and remove fire-stain and solder marks. As each grade of emery paper is used, change the sanding direction by 45 degrees so that the previous marks are visible to work away.

24 Once the final grade of emery paper has been applied, polish the card holder on mops.

Tip

On large flat surfaces, emery sticks offer even and stable pressure for removing fire-stain, excess solder, and solder marks.

Palladium Ring

This project is a fine example of how to utilize the hardness and brightness of palladium by applying it to a simple design, finished off with diamonds or lower-cost cubic zirconias or gemstones.

TOOLS AND EQUIPMENT

* Ring mandrel
* Rawhide mallet
* Flat nosed pliers
* Honeycomb board
* Liquid flux and clean brush
* Medium palladium solder
* Hand-held drill
* ¹⁄₁₆ in (1.5mm) and ¹⁄₃₂ in (0.7mm) drill pieces
* ¹⁄₃₂ in (1mm) and ¹⁄₃₂ in (0.7mm) burr pieces
* Two pairs of reverse-action tweezers
* Selection of needle files
* Selection of emery papers

SKILL LEVEL 👁👁

TECHNIQUES USED

* Multiple solder joins

Like platinum, palladium is recognized as a precious metal—but it has a much lower cost. Palladium has many of the same characteristics as platinum—such as hardness and brightness—but it is lighter, making it more comfortable to wear. Furthermore, the density of palladium is similar to silver or lower-karat gold, allowing for a greater range of complicated jewelry pieces to be achieved than with denser platinum.

The hardness and whiteness of palladium make it ideal for the setting of precious stones, be they colored gemstones or white diamonds. Its reflective qualities highlight and reflect the colors and purities of gemstones. It is also malleable and easy to bend. It can be cold worked without annealing. Of course, as with other metals, once the piece has been worked on, it will become work-hardened and annealing is required prior to further work on the piece.

MATERIALS:

Ring shank
2¼ in (57mm) of ⅛ x ¹⁄₁₆ in (3 x 1.6mm) rectangular palladium wire

Wires
2 pieces of ⅛ x ¹⁄₁₆ in (4 x 1.5mm) round palladium wire

Top section
¼ x ¼ x ¹⁄₁₆ in (8 x 8 x 1.7mm) palladium sheet

2¼ in (57mm)

⅝ in (17mm)

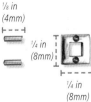

⅛ in (4mm)

¼ in (8mm)

¼ in (8mm)

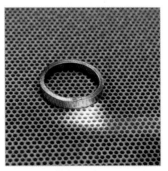

1 Form the annealed palladium wire for the ring shank around a ring mandrel. Make the ends meet very tightly and neatly with a rawhide mallet and flat nosed pliers if necessary. Palladium solder is not as smooth flowing as gold or silver, so be sure the seam is as tight fitting as possible.

2 Place the ring onto a honeycomb board and put a paillon of fluxed medium palladium solder on top of the ring seam. Although there is no need to flux palladium, it is used to hold the solder in position.

3 As the melting temperature of medium palladium solder is reachable with a standard torch, there is no requirement for special protective eye wear. Turn the torch to a fine oxidizing flame: very hot and precise, it will make quite a loud noise.

4 Using the high, intense heat from the torch, focus the flame around and just outside of the seam area. Unlike with silver, the heat should be directed around just the seam rather than the complete piece. Allow the piece to cool until no longer glowing (at least 2–3 minutes) before placing in water and pickle solution. The pickle solution might not remove the discoloration completely, but cleaning and finishing later will.

Tip

Keep the solder seam of the ring shank at the base. This will allow further soldering work to be distant from this join, but it also allows the piece to be sized if necessary at a later date.

5 Measure and mark the center point along two sides of the base of the central piece. Drill indentations into these marks but do not drill all the way through: approximately 1/32 in (1mm) depth is required. If necessary, extend the width of the holes with the 1/32 in (0.7mm) burr until the two wire pieces slot in tightly and securely.

6 Measure the top of the ring shank against the top piece drilled in step 5. Mark the position of the two holes and then drill matching indentations.

7 The two pieces of wire should fit both the top section of the ring and into the upper side of the shank.

8 Hold the ring shank in place with reverse-action tweezers on the honeycomb board. Place the first wire into one of the drilled holes. Heat the piece very slightly before applying a fluxed piece of palladium solder, which will stick in position.

9 Heat with a hot oxidizing needle flame, concentrating the heat only at the solder seam. There is no need to heat the entire piece. If the wire moves, keep it in position with a second pair of reverse-action tweezers. As solder flows, release the reverse-action tweezers, allowing the wire to solder in place.

10 Once the piece has been allowed to cool for at least 2–3 minutes, until no longer glowing, solder the second wire piece in place, again using two pairs of reverse-action tweezers. When soldering is complete, allow to cool before placing the piece in water and pickle solution.

11 Turn the piece upside down and insert the two wires into the holes on the back of the ring top. Place a piece of fluxed solder onto each wire piece, allowing it to touch both parts.

12 Apply heat from a small oxidizing needle flame. Concentrate on one solder seam first, then, when solder has flowed, take heat to the other. Allow to cool; quench and place in pickle solution.

13 Using needle files and emery papers, remove any excess solder and marks. This will also eliminate any surface discoloration that remained after immersion in the pickle solution.

14 Using the smaller drill piece, mark and drill holes before burring to the correct size for your stones. Set the stones and finish the ring by polishing, creating an attractive mirror finish.

This ring could easily be mistaken for platinum. But with a substantially lower cost, palladium is an attractive and competitive metal to use.

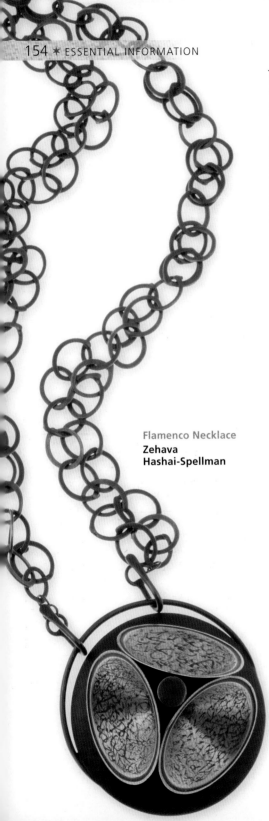

Flamenco Necklace
**Zehava
Hashai-Spellman**

Essential Information
Properties of Solders

SILVER SOLDERS		
Type	Use	Flow temperature
IT/enameling	Use only if piece is being enameled.	1346–1472°F (730–800°C)
Hard	Always use first.	1373–1432.4°F (745–778°C)
Medium	Use at intermediate stage. Can be sticky.	1328–1392.8°F (720–765°C)
Easy	Use only as a last resort or for soldering a piece when the solder grade history is unknown.	1301–1333.4°F (705–723°C)
Extra easy	This should only be applied if local solder seams are at risk of reflowing and causing unwanted movement in the construction.	1232.6–1308.2°F (667–709°C)

GOLD SOLDERS		
Type	Use	Flow temperature
22-karat	Use only with 22kt gold.	Available in Hard, Medium, and Easy. Melting temperatures range between 1590.8–1760°F (866–960°C).
18-karat	Use only with 18kt gold. The melting temperatures given are for yellow gold solder. Different colors of 18kt gold solder have varying melting temperatures.	Hard: 1455–1525°F (790–830°C) Medium: 1346–1392.8°F (730–765°C) Easy: 1290–1320°F (700–715°C)
14-karat	Use only with 14kt gold	Hard: 1382–1445°F (750–785°C) Medium: 1344.2–1439.6°F (729–782°C) Easy: 1310–1346°F (710–730°C)
9-karat	Use only with 9kt gold. The melting temperatures given are for yellow gold solder. Different colors of 9kt gold solder have varying melting temperatures.	Hard: 1390–1465°F (755–795°C) Medium: 1355–1390°F (735–755°C) Easy: 1202–1328°F (650–720°C)

Properties of Metals

	Metal	Alloy composition (parts per thousand)	Color	Melting point	Specific gravity
Gold	24kt (fine) gold	999 parts gold	Rich yellow	1945°F (1063°C)	19.5
	22kt gold	920 parts gold (alloyed with silver and copper)	Dark yellow	11769°F–1796°F (965°C–980°C)	17.8
	18kt gold	760 parts gold (alloyed with proportions of silver, copper, zinc, and palladium)	Yellow, red, white, green	1607°F–2399°F (875°C–1315°C)	15.2–16.2
	14kt gold	585 parts gold (alloyed with silver or palladium, copper, and zinc)	Yellow, white	1526°F–2372°F (830°C–1300°C)	13–14.5
	9kt gold	375 parts gold	Pale yellow, red, white	1616°F–1760°F (880°C–960°C)	11.1–11.9
Silver	Fine silver	999 parts silver	Lustrous white	1762°F (961°C)	10.5
	Britannia silver	958 parts silver / 42 parts copper	White	1650°F–1725°F (900°C–940°C)	10.4
	Sterling silver	925 parts silver / 75 parts copper	White	1480°F–1740°F (805°C–950°C)	10.3
Platinum/ Palladium	Fine platinum	999 parts platinum	Gray-white	3227°F (1775°C)	21.4
	Platinum	955 parts platinum / 45 parts copper	Gray-white	3173°F (1745°C)	20.6
	Palladium	950 parts palladium (gallium, copper)	White	2462°F–2552°F (1340°C–1400°C)	11.7
Base metals	Copper	999 parts copper	Warm orange	1480°F–1980°F (804°C–1082°C)	8.94
	Brass	670 parts copper / 330 parts zinc	Pale yellow	1690°F–1760°F (921°C–960°C)	8.5
Ferrous metals	Stainless steel	800–900 parts iron / 100–200 parts chromium	Gray-white	2642°F (1450°C)	7.8

Table of ring sizes

U.S.	U.K.	Europe	Ring blank length* (mm)	Ring blank length* (inches)	Inside diameter (mm)	Inside diameter (inches)
½	A	38	40.8	1.61	12.1	0.47
1	B	39	42.0	1.65	12.4	0.49
1½	C	40.5	43.2	1.70	12.8	0.50
2	D	42.5	44.5	1.75	13.2	0.52
2½	E	43	45.8	1.80	13.6	0.54
3	F	44	47.2	1.85	14.0	0.55
3¼	G	45	48.3	1.90	14.2	0.56
3¾	H	46.5	49.5	1.95	14.6	0.57
4¼	I	48	50.8	2.00	15.0	0.59
4¾	J	49	52.7	2.05	15.4	0.61
5¼	K	50	53.4	2.10	15.8	0.62
5¾	L	51.5	54.6	2.15	16.2	0.64
6¼	M	53	56.0	2.20	16.6	0.65
6¾	N	54	57.8	2.25	17.0	0.67
7	O	55.5	58.4	2.30	17.2	0.68
7½	P	56.5	59.5	2.35	17.6	0.69
8	Q	58	60.9	2.40	18.0	0.71
8½	R	59	62.3	2.45	18.4	0.72
9	S	60	63.4	2.50	18.8	0.74
9½	T	61	64.8	2.55	19.2	0.76
10	U	62.5	65.9	2.60	19.6	0.77
10½	V	64	67.4	2.65	20.0	0.79
11	W	65	68.6	2.70	20.4	0.80
11½	X	66	69.9	2.75	20.8	0.82
12	Y	68	71.2	2.80	21.2	0.83
12½	Z	69	72.4	2.85	21.6	0.85

Some useful measurements

Standard sizes of:	mm	inches
Diameter of earring posts and wires	0.8–0.9	0.031–0.035
Necklace lengths	400	16
	450	18
	500	20
Bracelet lengths	175	7
	190	7.5
	200	8.5
Bangle diameters	60	2.4
	65	2.6
	70	2.8

GEOMETRY FORMULAS

- **To find the circumference of a circle from the diameter:** Circumference = 3.142 x diameter
- **To find the circumference of a circle for a ring, bezel, or bangle:** Circumference = 3.142 x diameter + thickness of the metal.
- **To find the area of a circle:** Area = 3.142 x (radius²)
- **To find the diameter of a circle used to make a dome:** Outside diameter of sphere minus thickness of metal x 1.43 e.g., 18 mm o.d., 0.6 thickness: 18 – 0.6 = 17.4; 17.4 x 1.43 = 25mm
- If less accuracy is required, add the diameter of the dome to its height to find the approximate diameter of circle needed.

Using ring blank measurements

Always add the thickness of the metal you are using to the length of the ring blank * required for a particular size, to ensure accurate results. When measuring a finger, use a measuring gauge that is a similar width to the ring you are making—a wide band ring will need to be a larger size to fit over the knuckle than a thin band.

Index

Credits

Quarto would like to thank the following for kindly supplying images for inclusion in this book:

Agnew, Katherine, www.katherineagnew.com, p.15bl

Akinshin, Ilya, Shutterstock.com, p.39bc

Alexander, Dauvit, The Justified Sinner, www.justified-sinner.com, pp.2, 17tr, 19tr

Bone, Allyson, www.allysonbone.com, Photo: Allyson Bone, p.13tl

Courtesy of Abigail Stradling, www.abigailstradling.co.uk, p.64bl

Devenney, Wing Mun, www.ispymagpie.com, pp.17tl, 19br, 62bl

Evans Jeweller, Will, www.willevansjeweller.com, p.78b

Feather, Robert, www.robertfeatherjewellery.co.uk, pp.18bl, 54bl

Georgeiopoulou, Sophia, Goldsmith at Kosmimata, www.kosmimata.com, pp.16br, 19tl

Gowans, Jane, www.janegowans.co.uk, Photo: What Kristen Saw, p.68

Hashail-Spellman, Zehava, www.zhs-studio.com, Photo: Richard Valencia, pp.5, 13br, 154

High, Charlie, www.charliehigh.com, p.83cl, p.96br

HS Walsh, www.hswalsh.com, pp.34bl, 35r, 36tl, 37tr

kritskaya, Shutterstock.com, p.32b

Laird, Ruth, www.ruthlaird.com, p.14br

Lees, Katie, www.katieleesjewellery.com, p.91tr

Logan, Amy, www.amylogan.co.uk, Photo: Mike Briggs, p.13bl

London Silversmithing, Helen, www.helenlondon.co.uk, Photo: Ian Thwaits, p.14tr

Lühl, Frieda, www.frieda.co.za, Photo: Leah Hawker, www.leahhawker.co.za, p.18br

Markwick, Jo, www.kalojewellery.co.uk, p.52b

McCullagh, Jonny, Shutterstock.com, p.39br

McCulloch, Fiona, fionnebrown.co.uk, Photo: Neilson Photography, p.14bl

McGovern, Lisa, www.allpreciousthings.co.uk, p.16tl

Moore Jewellery, Laura, www.lauramoorejewellery.co.uk, p.15tr

Morrison, Nicola, www.nicolamorrison.co.uk, Photo: Shannon Tofts, p.16bl

Newell Price, Cathy, www.cathynewellprice.co.uk, Photo: Keith Leighton, p.160

Nuell, Mark, www.marknuell.com, Photo: Peter White FXP Photography, p.66bl

Oliveira, Filipa, www.filipaoliveirajewellery.com, p.17br

Perridge, Drew, www.drewperridgejeweller.co.uk, p.14tl

Peters, Felicity, www.felicitypeters.com, Photo: Victor France, pp.3, 12t, 15br

Pino, Claudio, www.pinodesign.net, Photo: Claudio Pino, pp.1, 12br

Potter, Suzanne, www.suzannepotterjewellery.com, pp.19bl, 60bl

Poupazis, Chris & Joy, www.cjpoupazis.com, Photo: Chris Poupazis, p.72b

Rezac, Suzan, www.suzanrezac.com, pp.9, 13tr, 141b

Richardson, Mark William, Shutterstock.com, p.39t

Saito, Kayo, www.kayosaito.com, p.18tr

Sutton Tools, www.suttontools.co.uk, pp.22, 23, 24

Swift, Leila, www.leilaswift.com, p.18tl

Tavender Jewellery, Faith, www.faithtavender.com, Photo: Full Focus, p.8b

Thomson, Inness, www.innessthomson.wix.com, p.8t

Thomas, Mari and Emma Sedman, p.83bl

Tonkin, Cara, info@caratonkin.com, www.caratonkin.com. p.17bl

Tosto , Alexandra, www.alexandratostodesign.co.uk, p.15tl, Photo: Simon B. Armitt, p.12bl

Wiseman, Georgia, www.georgiawiseman.com, p.4

Zucchi—Italy, Melania, www.melaniazucchi.com, p.16tr

All step-by-step and other images are the copyright of Quarto Publishing plc. While every effort has been made to credit contributors, Quarto would like to apologize should there have been any omissions or errors— and would be pleased to make the appropriate correction for future editions of the book.

AUTHOR AKNOWLEDGMENTS

To my boys, Jason, Dylan, and Rhys, thank you for putting up with the sleepless nights, tantrums, and the tears. Without the help of my boys and Loi Tai Wong, Tung Pui Wong, Ho Wai Wong, and Liz Devenney, the writing of this book would have been impossible.

A special thanks to Inness Thomson, (innessthomson.wix.com/jewellery), whose outstanding manufacturing skills produced the majority of the samples pieces in the book following my designs and often somewhat ambitious technical notes.

To Dauvit Alexander (www.justified-sinner.com), David Webster, Fiona Mc Culloch (fionamcculloch.co.uk), Jim Davidson, Kath Duncan (www.kddesignsjewellery.co.uk), and Gordon Stewart of North Glasgow College who all offered support and technical advice, as well as the use of their fantastic facilities. Nigel Munro, Lisa McGovern (www.allpreciousthings.co.uk), and Jo Markwick (www.kalojewellery.co.uk).

Lily de Gatacre, Susi Martin, and Phil Wilkins from Quarto, who made this experience as enjoyable and stress-free as possible.

Jamie Hall (ganoksin.com/blog/primitive) who supplied the historical information required for the introduction.

Liz Olver who not only directed me to this opportunity but offered the most valued advice and support at one of the most crucial moments in my jewelry career.

Bairds of Glasgow www.goldline.co.uk/contactPage.page

FURTHER INFORMATION

The information supplied in this book is accurate and true to the best of my knowledge. All safety procedures have been considered but we cannot guarantee avoidance of any injuries that may occur while using the techniques in this book. Jewelry-making poses some dangers. It is at the reader's own risk to follow and apply the techniques demonstrated.